A Second Helping of Murder

Also by Jo Grossman and Robert Weibezahl

*A Taste of Murder: Diabolically Delicious Recipes
from Contemporary Mystery Writers*

*Jo Grossman and Robert Weibezahl are donating a portion of their profits
from this book to From the Wholesaler to the Hungry, a national organization that helps cities across the country develop systematic programs to
distribute nutritious, fresh produce to low-income adults and children.*

A Second Helping of Murder

More Diabolically Delicious Recipes from Contemporary Mystery Writers

Jo Grossman   Robert Weibezahl

Poisoned Pen Press

Poisoned
Pen
Press

Library of Congress Catalog Card Number: 2003110517

ISBN: 1-59058-077-X

Poisoned Pen Press
6962 E. First Ave. Ste 103
Scottsdale, AZ 85251
www.poisonedpenpress.com
info@poisonedpenpress.com

Printed in the United States of America

Cover Design: J.J. Smith-Moore
Interior Design: The Printed Page

ACKNOWLEDGMENTS

As Janet Rudolph recently wrote in an issue of *Mystery Readers Journal* devoted to Culinary Crime, the detective like the cook organizes chaos into order. The same might be said for those foolhardy enough to undertake a cookbook such as this one. Of course, unlike those self-reliant detectives, we never could have done it without the help of many friends and colleagues, and we would be remiss if we did not thank some of them while we have the opportunity.

For advice, both editorial and culinary, we are indebted to Lucy Rochambeau, Lucille Bralower, Betty Froelich, Arline Reilly, and Kathy Kamiya. Marcy Reed cheerfully allowed herself to be conscripted as our proofreader and Katie Weibezahl provided some invaluable clerical help. Many folks helped spread the word about the new book—in fact, in the anonymous age of e-mail we can't even be certain who they all were—but we know that a few of our biggest boosters were Jerrilyn Farmer, April Henry, Janet Rudolph, Kate Mattes, and the indefatigable Susan Richman. And special thanks to Nathan Walpow for creating and hosting the webpage for *A Taste of Murder*.

So many of the contributors to *A Taste of Murder* helped with promotion of that book, and we're afraid if we tried to thank all of them individually we would leave some out. So, forgive us for a blanket expression of our heartfelt thanks to all of you, and thanks in advance to the contributors to this volume who no doubt will step up to the publicity plate with the same gusto.

Thanks to everyone at Poisoned Pen Press, including Barbara Peters, Jennifer Semon, and especially Robert Rosenwald for his unerring enthusiasm and good taste. Kudos, too, to Lisa Liddy and J.J. Smith-Moore for their bang-up design of both the inside and the cover of the book.

We save the greatest thanks to last, of course—to all the generous mystery writers who contributed recipes, it goes without saying that we couldn't have done it without you. The most wonderful thing about putting together both volumes has been getting to know you all, and we are grateful for the pleasure of your company.

Contents

Introduction

The Set-Up

A Shot In The Dark

In The Soup

Crumby Situations

A Brunch Of Crooks

The Quick And The Dead

A Criminal Past-a

Red Herrings

Murder Most Fowl

Meating Out Justice

No Bone To Pick

Accomplices

Tough Cookies

The Proof Is in the Pudding

INTRODUCTION

Dishing Up Another Serving of Crime and Nourishment

When we first had the idea of putting together a cookbook featuring recipes from both today's mystery writers and classics of crime, we knew we had stumbled onto something clever and fun. But we had no idea what an incredible response *A Taste of Murder: Diabolically Delicious Recipes from Contemporary Mystery Writers* would receive from the mystery community. Unofficially "launched" at Bouchercon in September 1999, every copy the dealers had brought to Milwaukee was sold by 1 o'clock the first day. Much time was spent that weekend apologizing to those fans who hadn't been able to snag a copy. Beyond that initial hitch, though, the future was bright for *A Taste of Murder*. The book became an informal autograph album for mystery lovers and, even four years later, many of the contributors report that they still are asked to sign their recipes when they give a reading.

Almost from the start, folks have asked if there would be a follow-up volume. Gracious authors who had missed their first chance to contribute wanted to take part, and lots of fans were not shy about telling us who they hoped to see the next time out. Due to the vagaries of the publishing world, the project languished for a time, until Poisoned Pen Press came to the rescue and agreed not only to publish a new volume, but to return *A Taste of Murder* to print as well.

So, herewith *A Second Helping of Murder: More Diabolically Delicious Recipes from Contemporary Mystery Writers*. The title says it all, and we believe that these newly assembled recipes from mystery writers rival those in volume one. Though more than a few of the contributors from last time offered to provide us with new recipes, we had to decline their generosity, believing that fans wanted a whole new stable of authors. (There is one exception to this rule, and we leave it to you experienced mystery readers to discover which one author is in both books—and why.) Hope your own favorite is on board.

As was the case with *A Taste of Murder*, a portion of the royalties from this book will be donated to From the Wholesaler to the Hungry. Our association with this outstanding charity happened quite serendipitously. From the start it seemed to make more sense to give some of the profits to a food-based charitable organization, rather than doling out a minuscule and inconsequential honorarium to each mystery writer who contributed a recipe. We approached one nationally-known group with the idea and were told that *they* would need to approve *us*. That hardly seemed like the smartest way for them to conduct their fund-raising, so we cast about for an alternative. A well-timed article in the *Los Angeles Times* about From the Wholesaler to the Hungry was intriguing. Then a week later, quite by chance, our then-agent mentioned that she knew these two people who were doing great work providing produce to the needy....Yup, you guessed it.

Those people are Peter Clarke and Susan Evans of the University of Southern California School of Medicine, and the creators of From the Wholesaler to the Hungry. Their mission is to get produce into the hands of low-income children and adults, and they do this by helping cities and rural communities around the country set up permanent programs that channel unsold produce from distributors to food banks. Since they started the program in 1991, they have set up programs in 134 cities, and they continue to expand their reach, most recently moving into areas of Appalachia. They are also instituting a pilot program that will match each food bank client with his or her specific needs, even providing recipes for how to serve or prepare the food for optimal nutritional value.

Unlike most charities with such a broad reach, From the Wholesaler to the Hungry operates on a shoe-string. And while our modest contribution to their good work cannot match a large corporate or foundation grant, we hope that anything we provide will aid Susan and Peter in their grass-roots efforts to help the less privileged among us eat nutritiously and well. If you would like more information about the program, please contact them at: Keck School of Medicine, University of Southern California, Institute for Prevention Research, 1000 South Fremont, Unit 8, Alhambra, California 91803. Tax-deductible contributions can also be sent to this address. E-mail can be directed to shevans@usc.edu or chmc@usc.edu.

Since publishing *A Taste of Murder*, we have sat on a number of panels at mystery conferences where the topic was culinary mysteries. The operative question is always: Why this link between food and crime fiction? By now, we've postulated with the best of them, and come up with the usual stuff. Assembling the clues to solve a crime is like putting together a recipe. Food provides comfort during trying times (is anything more trying than having to solve a murder?). What your favorite sleuth eats is a reflection of his or her soul. Social gatherings, which invariably involve food, are an awfully good place to bump someone off. And, quite simply, food is a heck of a convenient place to plant the poison.

Whatever the reason, there is no denying that many of us enjoy our murders with a little food on the side. The recipes in *A Second Helping of Murder* have been gathered with just that taste in mind. So, enjoy serving up some of the specialties of your mystery-writing favorites. Our fondest hope is that you have half as much fun reading, testing, and tasting as we did putting together this collection of recipes to die for. As you venture into the kitchen, though, we ask but one thing: Please remember to let the nourishment fit the crime.

THE SET-UP

Ali's Babaganough

ELIZABETH PETERS

*T*here is truly nothing quite like authentic Egyptian food. And, say what you will, it is not the same here as it is in Egypt; perhaps it is the fresh spices purchased in the open air spice market, or the land, or even the company I keep when I visit, but nothing matches the experience of eating it there. If Egypt's monuments, its terrain, and my dear friends were not enough of an allure—the food surely would be. Five years ago I visited the Hierakonpolis expedition (south of Luxor) and was treated to Babaganough made by the field cook Ali (unlike Amelia's Mahmud, this fellow is not only an excellent chef but extremely pleasant natured as well). I have never tasted anything like it before or since. After numerous requests, he gladly shared his recipe with everyone through the *Nekhen News* bulletin. However, I have not attempted to make it as I know anything I make will merely be a let down to the memory of that wonderful meal. I will simply have to go back—such a trial!

Take 2 medium to large purple eggplants (aubergine) and bake at 350 degrees for 30 minutes, or toast them in a small frying pan (or a tin coffee can lid, which actually works better) over medium-high heat until soft all over and the skin is slightly singed. Peel the eggplant; the skins should fall away easily from the softened pulp. Place the pulp on a plate and mash lightly with a fork, or use a food processor if you prefer.

Squeeze 3 small (or 1 large) lemons, and mix the juice with the eggplant pulp. Add plain liquid *tehina* (available from any Middle Eastern grocery store); a small amount will do. Mix in increasing amounts of *tehina* until the mixture gets stiff, adding water or more lemon juice to thin and soften the mixture to the desired consistency. Add a pinch of ground cumin to taste and then add anywhere between 2 and 10 crushed cloves of garlic, depending on your taste (I like it hot!).

Top with parsley. Serve with pita bread, raw vegetables, salad, felafel or kofta (meat balls).

Barbara Mertz, better known in some circles as Elizabeth Peters, is the author of over thirty mystery novels, many of which make use of her academic training as an Egyptologist. Her most popular series has followed the career of Victorian female archeologist, Amelia Peabody Emerson, and her eccentric family, from 1884 to—thus far—1919. She has received many awards, including Grand Mastery by the MWA and the Lifetime Achievement award from Malice Domestic.

Maxi's Hot Artichoke Dip
KELLY LANGE

*H*aving been invited to submit an example of my culinary skills, such as they are, my character Maxi Poole and I humbly offer our favorite party dip recipe.

This comes, however, with a caveat. You see, I don't cook, and neither does my sleuth, Maxi Poole. You'll find this clearly stated in a verbatim quote from the first chapter of my latest Maxi Poole mystery novel, *Dead File*:

"Maxi's father was a pharmacist who put in long hours navigating the small east coast chain of drugstores he owned, and had never been concerned with dinner being on the table at any special time, and her mother was a dance instructor who still maintained her dancer's lean body. Except on holidays, food was never much of an issue with the Pooles, and in fact nobody in the family was a particularly good cook, Maxi included. They joked about that. Take-out, both plain and fancy, was king at their New York brownstone."

Now, having admitted that Maxi and I don't cook, let me hasten to add that we definitely and most certainly do entertain. So herewith, our recipe for delicious hot artichoke dip, which is easy to make and absolutely crowd-pleasing delicious.

> 1 cup mayonnaise
> 1 cup grated Parmesan cheese
> 1 cup cubed Swiss cheese
> 1 can artichoke hearts, diced
> 1 teaspoon garlic powder
> Salt & pepper to taste

Mix together and pour into a shallow baking dish. Bake at 350 degrees for 30 minutes.

Serve with crackers or crusty bread (and wine).

Kelly Lange was the first woman television reporter to become news anchor on any of the NBC-owned stations in the country. Her sleuth, Maxi Poole, is also a television reporter-anchor. In fact Maxi is very much like Kelly, except she's taller, thinner, younger, sexier, and blonder. The Maxi Poole mystery series includes *The Reporter* and *Dead File*. Lange is also the author of two other mystery novels, *Trophy Wife* and *Gossip*.

Rueben Dip

TAFFY CANNON

I first encountered this about ten years ago on a Thanksgiving visit to relatives in the Midwest. I sat down beside a vaguely unattractive dip, surrounded by pieces of rye bread. After one taste, I was in love. They had to pry me away for the real dinner.

Since then, I've served this at our annual Christmas Open House. Because the proportions remain the same no matter how much or how little you make, I make enormous quantities, up to three pounds of each ingredient. I have to mix it in a stock pot. I always tuck a bit away in the back of the icebox for later, because no matter how much I put out, it's always gone by the party's end.

> 8 ounces sliced corned beef
> 8 ounces Swiss cheese
> 8 ounces cream cheese
> 8 ounces sauerkraut, with juice

Chop the first 3 ingredients into the equivalent of ½-inch cubes and mix thoroughly. This is messy. Add the sauerkraut and mix some more. This is even messier. Place it in an oven-proof casserole and bake at 350 degrees for 20-30 minutes, until bubbling. Remove from the oven, and stir to mix in the cheese.

Serve with rye bread cut into 2-inch squares.

You can increase this as much as you want so long as you keep the proportions equal. Leftovers, if you should be so lucky, are microwavable.

Taffy Cannon, author of *Open Season on Lawyers,* also writes the Booked for Travel mystery series as Emily Toll.

Dellacasa's Spinach Dip

CYNTHIA LAWRENCE

$\mathcal{M}$y culinary mystery made its debut at the U.C.L.A. Book Fair. I was between writers offering chocolate chip cookies on one side, personalized fortune cookies on the other. I later retreated to my kitchen and, five added pounds later, had recipe cards to give away, based on what my heroine served from Dellacasa's catering kitchen. This spinach dip travels well, and it's fed many hungry readers at my book signings.

> 1 10-ounce package frozen chopped spinach
> 2 cups light sour cream
> 1 cup light or regular mayonnaise
> ½ cup chopped parsley
> 1 teaspoon dried dill seeds
> 3 teaspoons dry Italian salad dressing mix
> Salt and pepper to taste

In advance, thaw the spinach; squeeze it dry. Combine the uncooked spinach with the rest of the ingredients in a food processor or blender. Pulse until everything is well mixed, but still has some texture. You want to have colorful flecks of spinach and parsley.

Place in a covered container, and refrigerate at least 2 to 3 hours for flavors to blend.

Serve as a dip with raw veggies or tortilla chips.

Makes about 3 cups.

Cynthia Lawrence's heroine, hardworking caterer, Cat Deean, whips up tasty morsels in *Take-out City* and *Chill Before Serving: A Mystery for Food Lovers.* Cynthia is one of the editors of the Sisters in Crime anthology, *A Deadly Dozen.* She edited *The Thai Food Cookbook,* and is writing a mystery based on her trip to Thailand, the land of ancient temples and divine food.

Deviled Eggs
NERO BLANC

*A*s any fan of Nero Blanc's crossword mysteries knows, amateur sleuth and crossword editor, Annabella Graham, is addicted to deviled eggs; not to mention—it's the only item she knows how to cook!

Here then is "Belle" Graham's sinfully delicious recipe for a dozen of her "Eggs Tzaritza." Shell and slice lengthwise 6 hard-cooked eggs. Place the yokes in a mixing bowl and add: 4 ½ tablespoons of 27-Across, ¼ teaspoon of dried English 18-Down; then add freshly ground 10-Across and 6-Across to taste. With a fork, mash the yokes and mix well. Next fold in 1 ounce of drained 20-Across. Drop a healthy dollop of the yoke mixture into each of the dozen egg white with a 4-Down. Generously sprinkle 11-Down over the eggs and serve at 28-Across.

Across

1. Cream of the crop
6. Old tar
10. Pelt with shot
12. Lobster paw
13. *Lord Jim* star
14. "_____ Lama Ding Dong"
15. Aging chicken?
17. Grace ending
20. Pranks
22. Almond or cashew
23. Time, top or trade lead-in
24. Study
25. Author of *The Living River*
27. Star of *South Sea Woman*
28. Late afternoon
30. Lauria & Rather
31. London, Rome & Paris
35. Coffee containers
36. More steamy
37. Concept
38. Eliot's Marner

Down

1. Mil. address
2. Tennis call
3. NYSE notice
4. 3 wood
5. Apple splitter?
6. Currency
7. Tree shaded walk
8. Eel
9. Old flier; abbr.
11. Pricey eggs
16. Droll one
17. Anecdotes
18. Cut the _____
19. Stephen in Paris
21. _____-Cat
23. Hogwash
26. Carrara neighbor
27. 19-Down's thanks
29. Many CEOs
30. Post-party no-no
32. Vinegar's partner
33. Actors grp.
34. No, Dre & J

Nero Blanc's mystery series includes *Anatomy of a Crossword, A Crossword to Die For,* and *Corpus de Crossword.* Visit www.crosswordmysteries.com for more puzzles and books.

Answer Key

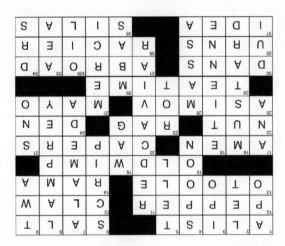

Sea-Deviled Eggs
DENISE DEITZ

*I*n *Footprints in the Butter,* an Ingrid Beaumont Mystery co-starring Hitchcock the Dog, Ingrid admits that she's not a very good cook. In fact, her favorite recipe is a peanut butter and banana sandwich—sliced and spread with a blunt knife. In her second mystery/adventure, Ingrid scores a movie that's being shot on Vancouver Island, B.C. She visits Canadian romance author, Victoria Gordon, who serves Sea-Deviled Eggs, a yummy aphrodesiac. Best of all, it's easy to prepare. Ingrid knows that her friend, diet club leader Ellie Bernstein, would approve, so she asks for the recipe.

> Sea Lettuce (*Ulva lactuca*)
> 6 hard boiled eggs
> Salad dressing (mayonnaise or low-cal mayo)
> Dijon mustard
> White pepper to taste
> Salt to taste

Crush two leaves of dried sea lettuce. Gently boil the 6 eggs; cool, shell, slice in half, and remove the yolks. Set the whites aside. Combine the yolks with salad dressing, mustard, white pepper, salt, and seaweed and mash well. Fill each white with the yolk mixture and refrigerate until ready to serve.

Gordon says: One can gather the brilliant green sea lettuce leaves from the rocks at low tide—in March and April. Wash only in sea water. Dry thoroughly and spread on paper towels. Can be crushed and stocked in salt cellars or spice containers. Use in cooking as you might use crushed and dried parsley. Very high in iron, protein, vitamins A, B, C, and other elements.

Denise (Deni) Dietz, considered a "culinary mystery author" because of her diet club series, is the author of *Throw Darts at a Cheesecake, Beat up a Cookie, Footprints in the Butter, Fifty Cents for Your Soul,* and *The Wishing Star.* She lives on Vancouver Island with her husband, novelist Gordon Aalborg (aka Victoria Gordon), and her two dogs: Sydney and Pandora. Visit www.denisedietz.com.

Laura Fleming's Heavenly Eggs
TONI L. P. KELNER

Some people call them deviled eggs, but Laura's Aunt Edna, a staunch supporter of Byerly's First Baptist Church, refuses to have anything to do with the devil. Besides which, these eggs are heavenly to eat. Heavenly eggs are also nigh about essential for sending anybody to heaven—nobody in Byerly, NC, would dream of having a funeral without serving Heavenly Eggs afterward.

And what with the increase in murders every time Laura comes home, there's plenty of opportunities to enjoy them.

> 6 hard-boiled eggs
> 3 tablespoons mayonnaise
> ¼ teaspoon yellow mustard
> ¼ teaspoon dry mustard
> ¼ teaspoon salt
> ¼ teaspoon pepper
> Paprika

Peel the hard-boiled eggs. (Eggs are the only things hard-boiled in Byerly). Cut them in half, lengthwise. Slip the yolks out, and lay the whites in your deviled egg plate. (What do you mean you don't have a deviled egg plate? Run out and get one before anybody finds out!)

Put the yolks into your Mama's old mixing bowl. (If you haven't inherited your Mama's mixing bowl yet, you can use your Grandmama's, or an aunt's. In an absolute emergency, you could buy a new one, but the eggs won't taste as good.) Use a fork to mash up the egg yolks, and then mix in the mayonnaise, yellow mustard, dry mustard, salt, and pepper. Spoon the mixture into the egg whites, and then sprinkle enough paprika on top to make it look pretty.

Cover the plate up, and put it into the refrigerator, but don't leave those eggs there for more than a day or they'll dry up. (In Byerly, that wouldn't be a problem, because there's always a funeral coming up.)

Toni L.P. Kelner serves up a heaping helping of Southern-style murder in *Death of a Damn Yankee*, *Mad as the Dickens* and *Wed and Buried*. Pay her a visit at www.tonilpkelner.com.

Furutani's Killer Gyoza
DALE FURUTANI

A gyoza is the Japanese first cousin of the Chinese pot sticker. Usually these ravioli-like delights are steamed and pan-fried, then served with soy sauce, vinegar and hot chili oil. This scrumptious variation is deep-fried to a golden, flaky morsel and served with smoky rich Hoisin sauce.

This is an original recipe developed by my wife Sharon (I cook, but usually from books). My contribution was to happily sample variations of the meat version until she got the recipe right. She's a vegetarian, so there's a veggie version that's also delicious.

This recipe makes approximately 20 gyoza. We serve them as an hors d'oeuvre, but with soup and rice they can also form the basis for a delicious Asian lunch.

> ½ pound boneless pork (in thin, small pieces. Look for pork *komagire*
>   if you have a local Japanese market)*
> ½ cup diced celery
> ½ cup diced onion
> ¼ teaspoon minced garlic (dried)
> ¼ teaspoon salt
> Bottled Hoisin sauce
> 20 gyoza skins **
> Vegetable oil for deep-frying

> *For vegetarian version: Substitute ½ pound of diced mushroom and 6 ounces of chopped, raw cashews for the pork)

> **If gyoza skins are not available locally, use wonton wrappers, which are usually available if a market has an Asian food section. Gyoza skins are round and wonton wrappers are square, but either will work.

Saute the celery, onions, garlic, salt, and pork pieces (or mushrooms and cashews in the veggie version). The pinkness should be gone from the pork and the vegetables should still be a little crunchy (which is why you want to use thin, small pieces of pork).

Place all the cooked ingredients in a food processor or blender, and finely chop the mixture to make a filling.

Take a gyoza skin and place a rounded teaspoon of filling in the middle. Brush water around the edge of the skin and press together to seal the edges. If you can get it, there is a gyoza press you can usually buy at Japanese markets to speed this process—it also crimps the gyoza skin edge into a beautiful rippled pattern!

After assembly, deep-fry the gyoza until they are a golden brown (about 2 to 3 minutes). Drain on paper towels.

Serve with Hoisin sauce for dipping. Plum Sauce can also be used as a variation. Both sauces can be found in the Chinese or Asian food section.

Best if served right after frying, when they are crispy and hot, but they can also be kept warm and served later if you don't let them get soggy.

Dale Furutani is the first Asian American to win mystery writing awards (an Anthony, a Macavity, and an Agatha nomination). *Publishers Weekly* has called him "a master craftsman." Among his titles are *Kill the Shogun*, *The Toyotami Blades*, and *Death in Little Tokyo*.

Maubi's Beef Patés (Pah-Tays)

KATE GRILLEY

At the annual St. Chris Agricultural Fair (the setting of *Death Lurks in the Bush)*, one thing you'll always find people eating as they stroll around the fairgrounds are patés, a turnover-type sandwich you can nibble from your hand. Maubi features patés year 'round on the menu of his Hot-to-Trot roach coach along with his famous homemade ice cream. Here's Maubi's special recipe:

Pastry

> 4 cups flour
> ½ teaspoon salt
> ¼ teaspoon baking powder
> 4 level tablespoons unsalted vegetable shortening
> 1 cup water

Place the dry ingredients in a large bowl. Cut in the shortening with two knives or a pastry blender. Add water gradually to form a soft dough. Knead gently on a floured board for a few minutes. Cover and let rest for about 10 minutes. Shape into small balls (about 24), roll each out, and cut them into the size circles desired for appetizer-size turnovers. (May also be served as a main dish and makes about 12.)

Filling

> 2 tablespoons butter or margarine
> 1 medium onion, chopped
> 1 clove garlic, crushed
> 1 pound ground beef
> 1 large green (sweet) pepper, chopped
> 1 tablespoon minced celery
> 1 tablespoon minced parsley
> ¼ cup tomato paste
> ¼ teaspoon oregano
> 1 tablespoon fine bread crumbs
> Hot pepper to taste (optional)
> Oil (for frying)

Sauté the chopped onion and garlic in butter or margarine, add the ground beef, and cook until the beef is browned (about 10 to 15 minutes). Add the remaining ingredients. Cook a few minutes longer. If filling seems too dry, add a little water.

Place a spoonful of filling on each circle of dough. Moisten the edge of the dough with water, fold the dough over the filling, and seal by pressing edge together with the tines of a fork. Fry in hot, deep fat until dough is golden brown and patés float in the oil (about 3 to 5 minutes). Avoid piercing the crust while the patés are frying so the filling does not come out of the turnover into the oil. Remove from the oil and drain on paper towels. Serve hot.

Makes approximately two dozen patés.

Note: Cooked (skinned) shredded chicken, or picked and boned leftover fish, or canned salmon, or ½ pound lean ground pork and ½ pound ground beef, can be substituted for 1 pound ground beef.

Also, patés can be baked in a moderate oven instead of fried. If baking, use a light egg wash (1 egg yolk diluted with 1 to 2 tablespoons water or milk, brushed on the top of the paté before baking) for a golden brown finished product. Bake until golden brown (about 10 minutes).

Virgin Islands resident Kate Grilley is the Anthony award-winning author of *Death Dances to a Reggae Beat*, the first in the Kelly Ryan/St. Chris Caribbean mystery series. Other books in the series include *Death Rides an Ill Wind* and *Death Lurks in the Bush*. Visit her at http://ourworld.compuserve.com/homepages/Kate_Grilley/.

Baked Brie with Macadamia Nuts
DEBORAH TURRELL ATKINSON

*T*his is a favorite hors d'oeuvre in my family. It's adapted from a recipe by Honolulu restaurateur Sam Choy, and it's extremely easy to prepare—and delicious. We have to shoo away the teenagers, as they inhale so quickly that the more dainty adult eaters (ha!) get only remnants. This would be a favorite *pupu* (the Hawaiian word for hors d'oeuvre) of Storm Kayama's, too, as she loves a good nibble and a glass of red wine.

Preheat oven to 425 degrees.

> Large round or wedge of Brie cheese
> ½ cup panko (a type of Japanese cracker crumbs) or ½ cup Ritz cracker crumbs
> ½ cup macadamia nuts
> 1 egg, beaten

Selection of the following:
> Lavosh (flat, Armenian-type cracker with sesame seeds) or Carr's water crackers
> Mango chutney
> Sliced apple (choose crisp ones, such as Granny Smiths or Gala)
> Red, seedless grapes

Blend the macadamia nuts and cracker crumbs together in a food processor, so that the macadamia nuts are finely chopped and mixed with the cracker crumbs. Coat the Brie thoroughly with the beaten egg, then dredge in the cracker/nut mixture until thickly coated. Place on an ungreased cookie sheet and put in the oven at 425 degrees for 10 minutes, or until crust is golden brown.

Put the cheese on a platter with the selected fruit, crackers, and chutney (if desired), and serve immediately with a good dry wine, or other cold beverage.

Deborah Turrell Atkinson writes the Storm Kayama series, including *Primitve Secrets*, set in the middle of the mystery and myth of Hawaii.

Bon Voyage Caviar Platter

MARY MARGARET NILAN

My first published novel, *The Buried Life*, is a tale of an innocent young heroine abroad in the deadly world of espionage. In the warm illusion of a romantic cruise, the heroine, who is on board by sheer accident, knows nothing of the cold reality of the high-stakes mission at sea. As events unfold, of course, she finds herself forced to try to solve the puzzle of the ill-fitting pieces. The personalities who surround her somehow do not exactly match what one would expect from officers, or crew, or even passengers on a small, upscale cruise in paradise. Why are areas of the ship, open to passengers on other pleasure vessels, strictly off-limits here? Odd events only deepen the mystery, leaving more unanswered questions.

In *The Buried Life*, my amateur sleuth is up against the skillful cunning of some of the best minds in the world of espionage. For her benefit, as well as protection of the ultimate secret, whenever a glint of truth might shine through one cover story, another must be produced. Conceal reality. This intricate spy-game must not be solved! So, in this cover world of champagne and caviar, my own "Bon Voyage Caviar Platter," which begins the mysterious cruise, is ideal for any cocktail party or large gathering. It is the answer when one might wish a bit of a unique presentation, either to have roving waiters offer guests, or to become the centerpiece of an intriguing table of hors d'oeuvres.

> ¾ cup sour cream
> 1 8-ounce package cream cheese at room temperature
> ¼ teaspoon chopped dill
> 2 cups finely chopped tops and bottoms of scallions
> 7 hard-cooked eggs, finely chopped
> 3 tablespoons mayonnaise
> ⅛ teaspoon white pepper
> ⅛ teaspoon salt
> 1 2-ounce jar black or red caviar; or 1 1-ounce jar of each
>   (drained and lightly rinsed)
> Parsley
> Assorted crackers or toast points

Line a 7-inch spring form pan with clear plastic wrap.

In a medium bowl, combine the sour cream and cream cheese until smooth. Spread half of the cheese mixture onto bottom of prepared pan. Sprinkle the chopped scallions and dill over the cheese mixture.

In a medium bowl, combine the eggs, mayonnaise, salt and pepper. Spread the egg mixture on top of the chopped scallions. Top with the remaining cheese mixture. Cover with plastic wrap and press gently to pack the cheese. Refrigerate overnight.

To serve, uncover and invert onto a chilled serving plate. Top with caviar which is spread to the edges.

Note: If both black and red caviar are to be served, cross 2 knives across the final cheese base to form an "X." Then fill in red caviar on the opposite triangles and black on the reverse triangles. Remove the knives, which then allows for neat separation between distinctly different caviars. Place the chilled serving plate in the middle of a larger serving platter, which is at room temperature, and place crackers and/or toast points in a circle surrounding the caviar. Garnish with parsley.

This serves many and is an ideal platter to be passed among guests while chilled flutes of champagne are offered at a bon voyage party or special reception.

Mary Margaret Nilan's, debut spy novel is *The Buried Life*. Visit her website at http://home.earthlink.net/~pnilan.

A SHOT IN THE DARK

Absolut Bawls
ELAINE VIETS

$\mathcal{M}$y character, Helen Hawthorne, is on the run after she comes home from work early one day and finds her handyman husband nailing their next-door neighbor, Sandy. Helen picks up a crowbar and…well, the next thing you know she's in South Florida, land of deadbeats, drunks and druggies. Helen, a former six-figure executive in staid St. Louis, now works minimum wage jobs in South Florida so her ex-husband and the court can't find her. In each book in the series, Helen and I work another miserable low-paying job. I've been a telemarketer, worked at a high-priced dress shop, and in book two of the series, a large chain bookstore. *Murder Between the Covers* features bookstore owner Page Turner, who drinks Absolut Bawls.

The current South Florida fashion at the clubs is to mix booze with caffeine-rich energy drinks, like Red Bull. This gives the party-hearty crowd a buzz that lets them dance till dawn. I used an energy drink called Bawls and created my recipe, Absolut Bawls. Bawls contains caffeine and Guarana, a Brazilian berry that has many unproven properties. Guarana is said to help with weight loss and enhance sexual performance. Brazilians use it in soda, candy and as a health drink. It's become hip in the US. Guarana is chemically similar to caffeine. The flavor is oddly appealing and slightly citrus-y.

> 1 sixteen-ounce bottle of Bawls, high caffeine Guarana beverage
> 1 to 1 ½ ounce shot of Absolut vodka
> Key lime (regular lime can be substituted)
> Ice

Fill a tall glass with ice and Bawls. Add the Absolut vodka to taste. Garnish with Key lime.

Elaine Veits writes two mystery series. The Dead-End Job series, described by Florida mystery writer Tim Dorsey as "Janet Evanovich meets The Fugitive," includes *Shop Till You Drop*, and mixes mayhem and humor, taking heroine, Helen Hawthorne, through many mysteries and an assortment of jobs—some of which Viets herself once filled. Her other series, featuring Francesca Vierling, includes *Rubout, Backstab,* and *The Pink Flamingo Murders.*

Barbados Heat

DON BRUNS

Barbados Heat was invented by a friend of mine in Barbados. First of all, a Caribbean drink has to have rum and tropical fruit, so we've started with a coconut rum base. And it has to have heat. The cinnamon flavor of the Goldschlager adds plenty of heat.

Barbados Heat, the book, features plenty of heat, including a raging fire that destroys a recording studio and kills a famous record producer and more. And the name of the book, just like the previous Mick Sever novel, *Jamaica Blue*, was the perfect title for a drink.

This drink, or a Jamaica Blue, is best consumed as you read the novels.

> 1 part coconut rum
> 1 part wild apple vodka
> 1 part cranberry juice
> Dash of Goldschlager

Shake with ice. Strain into a margarita glass.

Serves 1.

Mick Seaver appears in Don Bruns' first two mysteries, *Jamaica Blue* and *Barbados Heat*. Visit www.don-bruns.com.

Shaken, Not Stirred

James Bond doesn't utter those immortal words, "Shaken, not stirred," when he first introduces the world to his idiosyncratic martini in Ian Fleming's *Casino Royale*. But he is very explicit about the way the casino bartender should mix his particular variation:

> *"A dry Martini," he said. "One. In a deep champagne goblet."*
> *"Oui, Monsieur."*
> *"Just a moment. Three measures of Gordon's, one of vodka, half a measure of Kina Lillet. Shake it very well until it's ice-cold, then add a large thin slice of lemon-peel. Got it?"*

Bond's old friend Felix Leiter is astonished by the drink, and when Bond claims he's going to patent it as soon as he can think of a good name, Leiter suggests "Molotov Cocktail." Later, Bond settles on "The Vesper," in honor of the black-velvet-clad, raven-haired beauty Vesper Lynd.

The Vesper

3 measures Gordon's gin
1 measure vodka*
½ measure blond Lillet vermouth
Slice of lemon peel

Shake very well until it's ice cold. (Shaking makes the drink very cold and blends the gin and vodka well.) Garnish with a slice of lemon peel.

Serves 1.

*Some more advice from 007: *"If you can get a vodka made with grain instead of potatoes, you will find it still better."*

Poe Family Eggnog
ANNE POE LEHR

I'm very flattered to be asked to contribute one of Cousin Eddie's favorite recipes. Poe Family Eggnog has been a staple at Christmas for several generations at least. It is delicious, booze laden, and guaranteed to instantly clog all arteries. The original handwritten recipe was with papers in a secretary which has come down to her in the Poe family from at least 1790.

> 15 egg yolks
> 2 cups sugar
> A fifth of Napoleon Brandy
> ½ cup Jamaican Rum
> 1 pint whipped cream
> ½ cup cream
> 15 egg whites, beaten
> Nutmeg

Beat the egg yolks and gradually add the sugar. Continue beating until stiff. Very slowly add the brandy and rum to the yolk and sugar mixture. Add the heavy cream and whipped cream; stir. Fold in the beaten egg whites; chill.

Serve with a sprinkle of nutmeg on top.

The brandy "cooks" the eggs while the eggnog pickles the drinker.

Anne Poe Lehr, a cousin of Edgar Allan Poe, is the proprietor of Poe's Cousin, a bookseller specializing in mystery novels. You can visit at www.poescousin.com. Her relationship to Edgar is described on the website under "About Poe' s Cousin."

Pick-Me-Up On Noon Street

Think of a forties' private eye and what comes to mind? A trench coat and cocked fedora…a dimly-lit office in a not-so-great part of town (with a leggy, sharp-witted secretary out front, of course)…an overflowing ashtray on the desk….

And booze…a bottomless bottle of booze in the desk drawer. It's just amazing how that bottle is never empty, and there always seem to be a couple of semi-clean glasses at hand. Many a sorry tale from a dame in distress has been spilled over a glass of bourbon, or rye, or scotch.

Since so many key confrontations and important rendezvous take place at local bars, it's no wonder more than a few hard-boiled detectives fall from grace after hitting the bottle a little too often.

Take Raymond Chandler's Phillip Marlowe. In *The Long Goodbye*, he and troublemaker Terry Lennox head over to the bar at Victor's for a few rounds.

Terry likes to put on airs (*"You English?" "I've lived there. I wasn't born there."*), so it's hardly surprising that he has something to say about that classic English cocktail, the gimlet.

"They don't know how to make them here," he said. "What they call a gimlet is just some lime or lemon juice and gin with a dash of sugar and bitters. A real gimlet is half gin and half Rose's Lime Juice and nothing else. It beats martinis hollow."

"I was never fussy about drinks" is Marlowe's characteristically brusque response.

Not-So-Fussy Gimlet

Our research reveals that there is a lot of disagreement about how to make a proper gimlet. Some side with Lennox. But most seem to favor using more gin than lime juice. You can decide for yourself, but here's a traditional recipe for those who, like Marlowe, are not so fussy.

2 ounces gin
½ ounce (1 tablespoon) Rose's Lime Juice, or to taste
1 lime slice

Stir gin and lime juice well with ice (the taste of this drink benefits from a long stirring). Strain into a pre-chilled cocktail glass. Garnish with lime.

Some suggest that the glass can be sugar-frosted by moistening the rim with lime juice, then dipping in sugar. But, we're not so sure how our hard-boiled anti-hero would feel about that.

Serves 1.

In a letter to a Mr. D.J. Ibberson in April 1951, Chandler expounds a bit on the stuff Marlowe likes—and doesn't like—to imbibe.

"Marlowe's drinking habits are much as you state. I don't think he prefers rye to bourbon, however. He will drink practically anything that is not sweet. Certain drinks, such as Pink Ladies, Honolulu cocktails, and creme-de-menthe highballs, he would regard as an insult."

So what would Marlowe think about this potent creation we've named in his honor? With Chandler gone, we'll never know. But we like to think he would have found it the perfect mix of the hard and the sweet. Kinda like one of those blondes who is always stirring up trouble in his life.

Marlowe's Sweet Scot

1 shot scotch (the smoother the better)
1 shot Kahlua
Crushed ice
Glass swizzle stick (a must)

Put a fair amount of crushed ice into a highball glass. Pour in the shot of scotch. Pour in the Kahlua. Take the swizzle stick and give it a gentle twirl.

The tartness of the scotch blends surprisingly nicely with the sweetness of the Kahlua.

Raise the glass and toast Marlow and the rest of those fictional detectives who have entertained you!

Serves 1.

IN THE SOUP

Bubbie's Chicken Soup

(Submitted by Carlotta Carlyle)

LINDA BARNES

"Oh, the soup? You like it?"
"I love it. Would you give me the recipe?"
"Sure. Of course. An honor. You take a chicken and put it in the pot. Add some water."
"How much?"
"Enough."
"How big a chicken?"
"So it fits in the pot."
"And then?"
"You cook till it's done."

As you can tell from the above, my grandmother, she should rest in peace, was not eager to divulge her chicken soup recipe. Here, with a bit more detail, is the version my mother swears by—after years of sneaking into the kitchen to secretly observe my *bubbie* in action.

> 1 4- to 5-pound chicken (stewing fowl is okay, a broiler is fine, cut up chicken
>   parts will do in a pinch)
> 2 ½ quarts cold water
> A handful of fresh dill, chopped
> A handful of fresh parsley, chopped
> 1 medium carrot, diced
> 1 medium stalk celery, with leaves, diced
> 1 medium parsnip, diced
> 1 small onion, diced
> 1 teaspoon salt
> Pepper

Cover the chicken with the cold water, and heat the pot on high until it boils. Skim away scum that rises to the top (after about 10 minutes no more should rise). Lower the heat. Add the herbs and vegetables, and simmer for about 2 ½ hours. Taste and season.

When at the desired intensity, let cool and strain into glass jars or a smaller pot. Refrigerate overnight. Skim fat from the surface. Reheat and serve.

On Friday nights, my *bubbie* would serve this with *lukshen*, delicious thinly-sliced home-made noodles. On Passover, it came with matzoh balls big enough to sink a small ship, but those are a different story. A different recipe as well.

Linda Barnes is the author of ten Carlotta Carlyle novels, including *A Trouble of Fools*, winner of the American Mystery Award, *Snapshot*, and *The Big Dig*.

Shrimp Ceviche

K.J.A. WISHNIA

My character, Filomena Buscarsela, comes from Ecuador, where I lived for three years—also known as suffering for your art. Ecuador is a major exporter of shrimp. The freshest I ever had was in a fishing village near Machala where the shrimp were brought to the kitchen *still alive* in a bucket of water. This is a simple yet impressive recipe for when you don't really feel like cooking. In Ecuador, it takes hours to prepare because you have to peel and clean the shrimp by hand. But here—God Bless America!—we can buy them ready to serve.

Some people mistranslate *ceviche* as "shrimp cocktail." It's not. It's a cold shrimp and tomato soup eaten for breakfast, lunch or dinner. Ecuadorians swear it's good for a hangover, but of course I wouldn't know a thing about that. You can also substitute any other seafood for the shrimp. I've done it with sliced or cubed salmon and even canned tuna when especially rushed. It's also a great excuse to eat popcorn, another important Ecuadorian agricultural product.

> 1 pound shrimp
> 1 red onion
> 1 large tomato
> 2 juicy oranges (or about 1 cup of very pulpy orange juice)
> 2 juicy limes
> 2 tablespoons olive oil
> 4 tablespoons ketchup
> 2 sprigs cilantro
> 1 teaspoon salt
> ½ teaspoon pepper

Cook the shrimp (or your seafood of choice) in about 1 quart of water (Ecuadorian recipes are notoriously imprecise when it comes to measurements). Save the warm water. Slice the onion as thinly as possible and wash in hot water a few times to lessen the sharp taste. Drain. Place in a large serving bowl. Chop up the tomato and add to the bowl. Add the orange juice, lime juice, olive oil, ketchup, cilantro, salt, and pepper (see, I told you it was easy). Add the shrimp and a fair amount of the warm water to taste (it should be tangy but not too citric).

Serve with rice and popcorn on the side. Overthrowing government optional.

Serves 4.

¡Buen provecho, amigos!

k.j.a. Wishnia is the Edgar- and Anthony-nominated author of *23 Shades of Black, Red House,* and *Blood Lake,* all featuring Ecuadorian-American sleuth, Filomena Buscarsela.

Chicken Coconut Soup

LYN HAMILTON

*A*ntique dealer Lara McClintoch travels the world in search of rare objects for her store, finding murder and mayhem along the way. Never one to let a corpse or two spoil her appetite, she samples the local cuisine wherever she goes. While she neglected to mention it in her account of her most recent trip to Thailand, *The Thai Amulet,* she took a day off from sleuthing to attend the wonderful Chiang Mai Thai Cookery School where Sompon Nabian taught her to make a spicy soup very similar to this.

> 2 14-ounce cans unsweetened coconut milk
> 5 thin slices galangal or fresh ginger
> 4 shallots, chopped
> 5 to 10 or more small red chillies (Thai bird chillies if possible), cut into strips
> 2 stalks of lemongrass, lower third only, cut into 1-inch pieces
> 1 can straw mushrooms, or two cups fresh, cut in half
> 1 ½ cups skinless, boneless chicken breast, cut into strips
> 3 tablespoons Thai fish sauce
> 3 kaffir lime leaves, or 1½ teaspoons grated lemon or lime zest
> ½ cup chopped coriander (cilantro) leaves
> 2 tablespoons lime juice
> 2 spring onions, sliced

Heat the coconut milk in a wok on high heat. Add the galangal/ginger, shallots, chillies, lemongrass, and mushrooms, and bring to the boil, simmering for about 4 minutes. Add the chicken, fish sauce, and lime leaves/zest, and bring to the boil. When the chicken is cooked through, add half the coriander, turn off the heat, and stir in the lime juice. Make sure to remove the lemongrass before serving.

Serve garnished with remaining coriander and spring onions.

Lyn Hamilton's archaelogical crime series, featuring Lara McClintoch, mixes history, antiques and mystery. Among the titles are *The Etruscan Chimera, The Celtic Riddle,* and *African Quest.*

Cock-a-Leekie Soup

SUSAN KELLY

I dumped the soup into a saucepan and set it on the stove to reheat over a low flame. Then I put some cheese and crackers on a plate and set a place at the table. About five minutes later Jack wandered into the kitchen.

"Whatever it is you're making," he said. "It smells great."

"Thank you," I said. "It's an old Scottish recipe."

He got a beer from the refrigerator. "What's it called?"

"Cock-a-leekie soup."

"Yum," he said, uncapping the beer. "Sounds like a venereal disease."

"Yes," I said. "It's the tartan version of herpes."

—from The Summertime Soldiers

The British have a positive genius for giving their foodstuffs inane, unappetizing, or quasi-obscene names. Witness "toad-in-the-hole," "bangers and mash," "scrag end," "faggots and gravy," "stovies," "mushy peas," and the immortal "spotted dick," which, like "cock-a-leekie," sounds like nothing so much as an unfortunate medical condition. Translated, some of these dishes are actually palatable. Cock-a-leekie (chicken and leek) soup is more than palatable.

There are about fifty recipes for this soup. Some of them call for the addition of prunes, which sounds like a Celtic tsimmes. This recipe is my own.

1 ½ quarts chicken stock	¼ cup minced fresh parsley
¼ cup barley	1 clove garlic, minced
1 cup sliced carrot	1 sprig fresh thyme
1 cup sliced leeks (white part only)	2 cups diced cooked chicken meat
½ cup chopped onion	Salt and pepper
½ cup chopped celery	

In a large soup pot, bring the stock and barley to a boil. Lower the heat and cover pot. Simmer for ½ hour. Add the vegetables, parsley, garlic, and thyme. Return to a boil and simmer covered until the vegetables reach the desired degree of tenderness, about 15 minutes. Add the chicken. Simmer another 5 minutes. Remove the thyme sprig and discard. Salt and pepper to taste.

This soup keeps well if refrigerated in a tightly closed container, and may even be better the day after it is made, the flavors having had a chance to meld. Serve with a boule or baguette and a salad for a complete meal.

Susan Kelly is the author of the six Liz Connors novels, starting with *The Gemini Man* and ending with *Out of the Darkness*, and one non-fiction book, *The Boston Stranglers*.

John Marlin's Venison Chili Recipe
BEN REHDER

*J*ohn Marlin, the hero of my Blanco County comic mystery series, has been a game warden for twenty years. He spends his days checking deer camps and his nights chasing spotlighters. As you might guess, he works up a powerful hunger. There's nothing he likes better on a cold night than a big bowl of his own venison chili. Except maybe handcuffing a poacher.

      3 tablespoons vegetable oil
      1 large onion, finely chopped
      2 large cloves garlic, minced
      1 jalapeño, minced
      2 pounds ground venison (beef or lean pork will also work nicely)
      1 28-ounce can crushed tomatoes
      3 tablespoons red wine vinegar
      2 tablespoons Worcestershire sauce
      2 ½ tablespoons ground chili powder
      2 tablespoons ground cumin
      ½ teaspoon cayenne pepper
      2 teaspoons salt, or to taste
      1 large green bell pepper, seeded and finely chopped
      1 10-ounce can red kidney beans, drained
      3 tablespoons fine cornmeal, mixed with a little water into a smooth paste

Sauté the onion, garlic, and jalapeño in the vegetable oil over medium heat for about 5 minutes. Add the ground meat and cook, stirring with a wooden spoon, until the meat is no longer red. Drain the fat, if necessary.

Add all the remaining ingredients except the beans and cornmeal. Bring to a boil, then reduce heat to medium-low and cook uncovered for 30 minutes, stirring occasionally. The mixture should be fairly thick.

Stir in the beans and the cornmeal mixture and heat through.

Ben Rehder is the author of *Buck Fever* and *Bone Dry.* Visit him at www.benrehder.com.

Talbot's Three-Can Chili

DEBORAH MORGAN

$\mathcal{M}$y java-junkie sleuth, FBI-agent-turned-antiques-picker Jeff Talbot, isn't a cook. He has no reason to be, since his wife, Sheila, is a trained professional. But traumatic events have pushed her even further into her agoraphobia, and in the series' third novel, *The Marriage Casket*, she won't leave the couple's bedroom. In addition, she has turned to eating, rather than cooking, for comfort. In an effort to help, Jeff comes up with this three-can, four-minute wonder. He maintains that presentation is everything, and serves the chili in bowls from Sheila's yellowware collection, c. 1890. Oyster crackers on the side, of course.

> *Jeff twisted in bed so that he could get a clear view of the clock on Sheila's nightstand. Twelve-fifteen. He looked with envy at his sleeping wife, at the same time wondering why he was the only one suffering from indigestion. Both had eaten his most recent kitchen creation for supper, which Sheila had not only stamped with an enthusiastic approval but also had named "Talbot's Three-Can Chili."*
>
> *He had cooked up the quick and easy meal by opening three cans he had found in the pantry—one each of kidney beans (which he drained), Hormel's Vegetarian Chili, and Del Monte's Chili-Style Tomatoes. He hadn't told Sheila it was healthy, too, and saw it as a small contribution toward helping her cut back on calories.*
>
> *Now, he suspected that he was being paid back for trying to do a good deed. Taking care not to disturb Sheila, he slipped out of bed, grabbed his robe and a roll of antacids, and headed downstairs.*

In addition to *The Marriage Casket*, Deborah Morgan's antique-lover's mystery series includes *Death is a Cabaret*, which was nominated for a Barry Award and named Best Paperback Original of 2002 by *Deadly Pleasures*, and *The Weedless Widow*. You will find several of Chef Sheila's recipes at www.deborahmorgan.com.

Pumpkin Soup Masterpiece

SUSAN SLATER

This is a takeoff on my first novel *Pumpkin Seed Massacre* and damned good soup if I do say so myself. The Pumpkin Soup Masterpiece—a real killer but in a good way!

> 1 small to medium "pie" pumpkin
> 1 large onion chopped fine
> ½ teaspoon minced garlic
> 1 stick butter
> 3 cans beef broth plus ½ teaspoon of liquid bullion
> "Pinches" of rosemary, thyme, sage
> Dash of nutmeg
> Garlic salt to taste
> White pepper to taste
> ½ cup sour cream
> ½ cup half-and-half—more/less depending upon desired consistency
> Green onion, bacon, sour cream and chopped (salted) pumpkin seeds for garnish

Halve the fresh pumpkin, toss the seeds, and place cut-side down on foil in oven and bake 1 hour at 350 degrees. Scoop the flesh and puree in a blender. Set aside. Brown the onion in butter until "clear," with minced garlic, and add to the beef broth and herbs. Simmer for 15 minutes before adding to the pumpkin in the blender. Blend, then heat. Simmer for 30 minutes. Add garlic salt and white pepper to taste. Add the sour cream and half-and-half. Warm through but do not boil.

Serve in individual bowls with a sprinkling of chopped green onion, crumbled bacon, a dollop of sour cream, and chopped pumpkin seeds. Festive if served in small hollowed out pumpkin shells.

Susan Slater is the author of the Ben Pecos series *Thunderbird* and *The Pumpkin Seed Massacre*, which is the inspiration for this recipe.

Death Warmed Over
MARIA BRANDT

A nearly-forgotten gem from the golden age of mystery is Mary Collins, who wrote six novels between 1941 and 1949 before "retiring" to become a full-time mom. Her evocative titles include *Dog Eat Dog, Only the Good*, and *Death Warmed Over*.

In *Dead Center* (1942), Janet Keith ("Keith"), a young lady writer who hangs out with a bohemian crowd near San Francisco's famed Montgomery Block, is joined by Spike, the bodyguard hired by her posh parents to protect her after a woman has been murdered in a studio adjoining her own, for lunch at one of San Francisco's old-line restaurants. Hamish is Keith's pet Scottie.

> *Jack's is one of San Francisco's finest restaurants, but no one from the East would think so just to look at it. It is housed in a rather grimy, three-story building, the two top floors being devoted to private dining rooms. The restaurant proper on the first floor sports the usual San Francisco-beige walls interspersed with brightly varnished mahogany woodwork. The food is epicurean, and the service effortless. I had onion soup and celery Victor with crab legs. Spike had onion soup, a huge mixed salad, a steak approximately the same size as Hamish, a baked potato, two loaves of toasted French bread, and deep apple pie with plenty of cheese. All this was washed down with seven cups of coffee. I counted them.*
>
> *When Spike leaned back to smoke a cigarette with the final cup of coffee, he made a very profound remark which I shall cherish forever. "It takes lots of fuel to keep a big furnace goin'," he said.*

This culinary passage inspired *A Second Helping of Murder* to offer a recipe for the classic-style onion soup that patrons at Jack's might have enjoyed during the 1940s.

Golden Age Onion Soup

3 large onions, thinly sliced (about 1 ½ to 2 cups)
1 clove garlic, minced
3 tablespoons butter
4 cups vegetable stock (canned is fine, but homemade is better)
¼ teaspoon freshly ground pepper
4 slices French bread, thickly cut
4 ounces Swiss cheese, sliced
Grated Parmesan cheese

In a covered saucepan, cook onions and garlic in butter over low heat for 20 minutes, or until very tender. Stir occasionally. Add the stock and pepper. Bring to a boil, cover, and simmer 10 to 15 minutes.

While the soup is simmering, toast the bread slices. Place the 4 toasted slices on a baking sheet, and top each with sliced cheese and a healthy sprinkle of Parmesan. Broil until the cheese melts.

Ladle soup into 4 bowls, and top each with a toast slice. Serve with a nice chardonnay (much better than coffee!).

Makes 4 servings

You can find out more about Mary Collins at:
www.lib.berkeley.edu/~rbrandt/collins/index.html.

Murderously Good Maine Chowdah
LEA WAIT

*M*y grandmother's Maine seafood chowder is still one of my favorite suppers. Not only is it delicious, but it can be made in advance and then heated after a day at an antiques show, auction, or beach. In *Shadows on the Coast of Maine*, Maggie Summer visits her old friend Amy Douglas, and finds that chowder is a staple in a 1774 Maine house filled with mysteries, ghosts—and murder.

> 4 to 5 strips of bacon cut in small pieces
> ½ yellow onion per person, sliced and diced
> 3 garlic gloves, diced (add more if you love garlic!)
> 1 cup of chicken broth per person
> 2 medium white potatoes per person, pared and cut in 1-inch pieces
> Salt and black pepper to taste
> Tabasco sauce to taste
> ½ pound of fish (preferably haddock) per person, cut in ¾-inch pieces
> ½ pound of shrimp or lobster meat per person, also cut in ¾-inch pieces
> ½ cup light cream per person
> 2 tablespoons fresh chopped parsley per person

Heat the bacon in a 5-quart saucepan (or larger, if you're feeding all the local State Troopers). Add the diced onion and garlic, and stir over a medium heat until you can see through the pieces of onion. Pour in the chicken broth and add the potatoes. (If the broth doesn't cover the potatoes, then add water until it does so.) Add approximately ½ teaspoon salt, 1 teaspoon black pepper, and 2 to 3 teaspoons (depending on taste) of Tabasco sauce. Bring to a boil.

Reduce heat and simmer for about 10 minutes, or until you can stick a fork easily through a piece of the potato. Add the fish and shellfish. Cook another 5 to 10 minutes, until all is cooked. Then add the light cream and heat until hot.

Add the parsley, stir, and serve in bowls with plain chowder or "oyster" crackers, or with French bread.

Lea Wait, a Maine writer, is author of the "Shadows" antique print mystery series, starring Maggie Summer, including *Shadows at the Fair* and *Shadows on the Coast of Maine*. Visit www.leawait.com to learn more.

Journey to the Perfect Clam Chowder

YASMINE GALENORN

$\mathcal{M}$any years ago, when I was a child, my mother made her version of clam chowder. As much as I loved my mother, there is no way that I can honestly go on record and say she was a good cook. By the time I was twelve, I was out-gunning her in the kitchen. During my childhood, she would make 'clam chowder' for my stepfather. I wouldn't eat it, the stuff was vile. She would open a can of clams, add some reconstituted dried milk, and heat it up. Bingo. Clam chowder.

While my stepfather would reluctantly eat it, every Friday he'd go out to lunch and have clam chowder at a restaurant. As a child, I couldn't figure out why he bothered; the clam chowder Mom made was horrible and I couldn't for the life of me understand the attraction.

Finally, I moved away. At eighteen, I was halfway through my junior year in college, a long way from home, and paying my own way. I would occasionally go out to eat, even though my budget only allowed for soup or fish 'n chips. One day I stopped in at the café in the local Yardbird's store. I smelled something wonderful and asked the waitress what it was. "Clam chowder," came the answer.

Astonished, I decided to stretch my courage and give it another try. Maybe they knew something Mom didn't. When my order arrived, I stared at it in shock. The thick soup had potatoes in it! And celery! The chowder was creamy, not watery, with spices and herbs, and I even caught sight of a carrot or two. I polished it off, cleaning my bowl, wishing I had the money for another.

After that, at every restaurant I frequented, I would try the chowder, tasting the soup, attempting to identify the spices and herbs. A year or so later, I started working on my own recipe. I spent five years perfecting my version of clam chowder, and I wish my mother could have tasted it-boy would she have been surprised!

Finally, I came up with the recipe below, one of my favorites because it took me so many years to perfect, and because I love the taste of chowder. Now I'm on a new quest. No longer able to eat dairy, I'm experimenting with soy milk and soy creamer. But here's the original recipe, in all it's tasty wonder.

> 8 strips lean bacon
> 9 large red potatoes
> 2 tablespoons olive oil
> 1 bunch green onions, chopped
> ½ cup chopped yellow onions
> 4 cloves garlic, minced
> 2 teaspoons chicken bouillon paste, or 2 cubes chicken bouillon
> 1 teaspoon each: parsley, basil, tarragon, crushed black pepper
> ½ cup chopped celery
> 3 cans minced clams, not drained
> 2 cups half-and-half
> ¼ cup butter
> Salt to taste

Fry the bacon until crisp. Drain and crumble. Set aside.

Peel the potatoes and cube into ¼-inch cubes. Cover with boiling water (just barely cover the tops of the potatoes) and set over medium-high heat.

Add 3 tablespoons of bacon drippings to the olive oil, and heat over medium-high heat. Add the chopped green onions, yellow onions, garlic, bouillon paste, herbs, and celery. Sauté for 5 minutes. Add the clams (do not drain) and sauté another 5 minutes. Add the bacon and sauté 5 minutes more. Remove from heat.

When the potatoes are soft, drain, reserving 3 cups of the potato water. Mash about 1 cup of the potatoes, then add to the cubed potatoes, stir in the reserved potato water and half-and-half. Stir in the vegetable-clam mixture and butter. Heat through but do not boil. Salt to taste.

As good as this chowder is when freshly made, it's even better if you let it sit overnight (refrigerate, of course) and reheat again the second day.

Warning: This is not a low-fat food nor is it meant to be; I developed this recipe for taste and for taste alone! This recipe makes enough for an army, or at least a good-sized dinner party. If it's to be the main course, figure it will feed 6 to 8 hungry people, along with a salad and French bread or rolls.

Yasmine Galenorn is author of *Ghost of a Chance*, the first in the Chintz 'n China mystery series, along with numerous metaphysical titles. Learn more at www/galenorn.com.

Joe Wolf's Spicy Corn, Crab, and Squash Bisque
MARY ANNA EVANS

Joe Wolf Mantooth, a primary character in my novel *Artifacts*, is a skilled cook, but he's usually short on cash. This isn't much of a problem when it comes to ingredients—the Gulf of Mexico is full of fish, shrimp, and crabs, and God never made a vegetable that Joe couldn't grow. Unfortunately, his lack of funds also translates into a lack of electricity, and this is a constant culinary thorn in his side. If a dish can't be cooked on a camp stove, Joe doesn't get to cook it very often. And if an ingredient requires refrigeration, then he has to cook quickly, before it spoils in the Florida heat. Still, sometimes he catches a mess of crabs in the summertime, when his tomatoes are dead-ripe and his squash vines are overladen. On a lucky day like that, he digs deep in his pocket for a few dollars. He spends them on a quart of milk and a can of chicken broth and a dab of cream and invites his friends to dine like royalty. Heck, Joe's friends dine better than royalty. Neither the queen of England nor her chef has this recipe…but now you do!

4 tablespoons vegetable oil
2 medium yellow onions, diced
4 jalapeño peppers, seeded and minced
5 tablespoons flour
1 large can chicken broth (about 6 cups)
8 large tomatoes, peeled, seeded, and chopped
1 quart whole milk (4 cups)
½ teaspoon cayenne pepper
1 ½ teaspoon salt
¼ teaspoon pepper
3 cups fresh corn, cut off the cob (about 6 ears)
4 large yellow summer squash, diced
8 ounces lump crab meat
1 half-pint carton heavy cream (1 cup)

Heat the oil in a heavy soup pot. Add the onions and jalapeño peppers, and sauté until the onions are clear. Add the flour and mix well. Add the broth and tomatoes, and stir until the flour mixture is evenly distributed, then bring to a boil. Reduce heat to simmer. Add the milk, cayenne, salt, and pepper. Cover and simmer for 30 minutes.

Add the corn, squash, and crab meat and simmer for 10 minutes. Stir in the cream. Adjust seasonings and serve.

Serves 12.

Mary Anna Evans is the author of *Artifacts*, a Faye Longchamp archaeological mystery of Florida, past and present. Her website can be found at www.maryannaevans.com.

Tortilla Soup

CHARLENE TESS

While developing the character of Chico Martinez, the detective in *The Van Winkle Bride*, I visited many restaurants and locations along Mesa Street in El Paso, Texas, a street important to Chico's investigation. At one restaurant I ordered tortilla soup—just the type of lunch Chico would have enjoyed. It turned out to be fragrant, spicy, and absolutely delicious. I sent my compliments to the chef and a few moments later he materialized.

He said if he shared the recipe he'd get fired and besides it was for gallons of soup. But he winked at me began describing the ingredients used and the process. I scribbled it all on a napkin and after many refinements have perfected the recipe. It's a wonderful meal and turns out exactly right every time.

Chicken (1 small whole chicken or several chicken pieces)
6 small cans low sodium chicken broth plus 4 cups water
½ teaspoon white pepper
12 to 15 stalks celery, chopped into small pieces
Fresh cilantro leaves, chopped (I use ½ a bunch for a strong taste)

1 large yellow onion, chopped
1 large jar hot Salsa Victoria (it must be Salsa not picante)
White cheese (Jack or farmers)
1 dozen corn tortillas
Oil for frying
Salt
1 large ripe avocado
1 8-ounce carton sour cream

Boil the chicken until tender and falling off the bone. Cool, remove bones, and dice.

Prepare the chicken stock in a deep kettle or slow cooker. Simmer for 15 minutes or so while you prepare the other ingredients.

Add the white pepper, chopped celery, chopped onion, cilantro, diced chicken, and the salsa. Continue to simmer for approximately another 20 minutes.

Grate the white cheese.

Cut the corn tortillas into thin strips, and fry them in hot oil until crisp. Drain on a paper towel, and sprinkle with salt.

Peel and thinly slice the fresh avocado.

To serve: Fill a bowl with hot soup. Sprinkle white cheese on top. Garnish with a tablespoon of sour cream, avocado slices, and top with tortilla slices.

This recipe makes a spicy, delicious soup that will serve about 8. This is a healthy and tasty meal. And it's even better the second day when served as leftovers because the flavors blend.

Charlene Tess is the author of suspense novels *The Van Winkle Bride* and *Accidental Angel*. Find out more about her at her website, www.authorsden.com/charlenetess.

Tapper Lodge Chicken Soup

MARILYN MEREDITH

*T*his soup was served the snowed-in guests of Tapper Lodge located near the Giant Sequoias in the southern Sierra after the murder of one of the guests in the third Deputy Tempe Crabtree mystery, *Intervention*. This is the perfect soup to serve on a cold, winter night, or when your soul needs soothing. What's great about this recipe is that you can substitute almost any vegetable, and measurements don't have to be exact.

4 boneless, skinless chicken breasts
1 large can fat-free chicken broth
2 yellow onions, peeled and chopped
    (or you could use 2 bunches of green onions)
4 to 6 carrots, cut into rounds
1 bunch celery, sliced (I like lots of celery in my chicken soup—
    you might want less)
1 teaspoon chopped garlic
McCormick garlic and herb seasoning to taste
Salt and pepper to taste
1 cup cooked rice, or leftover cooked pasta

Using a large kettle, fill halfway with water, and add the chicken breasts. Cook until just done (no longer pink in the middle). Allow to cool, reserve the water.

Cut the breasts into ½-inch chunks, return the pieces to the water. Add the fat-free chicken broth. Add the onions, carrots, celery, garlic and seasonings. If needed, add more water. Cook over a medium heat until carrots are tender. Add the rice or noodles, and heat until hot.

Serve with crusty sourdough bread or biscuits.

Serves 8 or more.

Marilyn Meredith is the author of the Deputy Tempe Crabtree series, which includes *Deadly Trail, Deadly Omen*, and *Unequally Yoked*. Visit her at http://fictionforyou.com.

CRUMBY SITUATIONS

Archbishop Thoresby's Bread
CANDACE ROBB

*A*ctually it was called "Bishops Bread" as I was growing up, but I envision John Thoresby from my Owen Archer series, resplendent in white satin robes embroidered with gold thread, savoring this, my favorite Christmas confection, with brandywine after High Mass at York Minster. He would have found it a challenge to collect the ingredients in the 14th century, but what's life without mysteries? His cook Maeve surely would have enticed him with this "bread." Or perhaps Queen Phillippa would have rewarded his devotion with this treat.

Now my Scots sleuth Margaret Kerr would have washed down this treat with scotch whiskey-neat, of course. Her Uncle Murdoch, taverner and smuggler, would have had access to the highlanders' fiery "breath of life" if anyone did, and he would tell you that this bread goes best with a dash of fire. I agree.

But beware! The richness of the chocolate, the oil of the nuts, and the sweetness of the dates and cherries can serve to disguise a poison (optional) or two.

> 1 ½ cups sifted all-purpose flour
> 1 ½ teaspoon double acting baking powder
> ¼ teaspoon salt
> ⅔ cup semisweet chocolate pieces
> 2 cups chopped walnuts
> 1 cup snipped, pitted dates
> 1 cup halved candied cherries, ½ red, ½ green
> 3 eggs
> 1 cup granulated sugar

Start heating oven to 325 degrees. Grease well a 10-by-5-by-3-inch aluminum loaf pan, then line the bottom with heavy waxed paper.

Into a bowl, sift the flour, baking powder, salt; stir in the chocolate, nuts, and fruits.

In a large bowl, with an egg beater, beat the eggs; with a spoon, gradually beat in the sugar.

Fold the flour mixture into the egg mixture. Pour into the loaf pan. Bake 1 ½ hours, or until done. Cool the pan on a wire rack. If wrapped well, it keeps several days.

Makes 1 loaf.

Candace Robb's Captain Owen Archer and Thoresby can be found in her many medieval mysteries including *The Apothecary Rose*, *The Cross-Legged Knight* and *A Spy for the Redeemer*. Her newer series, also set in 14th century England, includes *A Trust Betrayed*. Learn more at www.candacerobb.com.

Killer Pumpkin Bread

JANET DAWSON

$\mathcal{I}$ don't remember where I got this recipe for pumpkin bread, but I have been making it for many years. Because I am the sort of cook who views a recipe as a jumping-off point, I have gradually refined and modified the recipe to make it my own, adding more spices, particularly cinnamon. I rarely measure the raisins or walnuts, preferring to toss in a handful.

It's a Christmas tradition for me to give loaves of this bread as gifts, so I often go into production mode, making double batches. Killer Pumpkin Bread starts with a Halloween tradition. I like all things pumpkin and that may have something to do with being born on Halloween (so was Dick Francis). I gave my character Jeri Howard the same birthday, just so I could remember when she was born. I even decorated my house for Halloween.

So when Halloween comes trick-or-treating, I pick out a small pie pumpkin. It has to be a nice round one with a good smooth surface for its "face," because instead of cutting it up for a jack-o-lantern, I draw a cat face on it, complete with ears and whiskers. Along about Thanksgiving, I cut up the Halloween pumpkin into small pieces, remove the innards (seeds and stringy stuff), then I boil the pieces until they are soft. After the pieces cool enough to be handled, I peel off the outer rind and puree the rest.

Fresh pumpkin makes killer pumpkin bread and it's wonderful plain or with cream cheese. Enjoy!

2 eggs, beaten
1 ¾ cup flour
1 ½ cup sugar
1 cup oil
1 cup pureed pumpkin, fresh or canned
¼ to ½ cup cold water
¼ teaspoon baking powder
1 teaspoon baking soda
½ teaspoon salt
2 teaspoons each: cinnamon, nutmeg, ginger, and cloves,
    or use more or less to taste
1 cup raisins
1 cup chopped walnuts

Preheat oven to 350 degrees.

Mix all the ingredients together well and bake in a greased loaf pan (or 2 small loaf pans) for at least 1 hour. Bread is done when a knife inserted in the middle comes out clean.

Janet Dawson is the author of the Jeri Howard series, which includes *Kindred Crimes, Don't Turn Your Back on the Ocean,* and *Nobody's Child.*

Bernier's Banana Bread
BETH SAULNIER

My heroine, Alex Bernier, may be a vegetarian, but she's a very hearty eater. One of her favorites is this moist, extremely tasty banana bread, which she uses to bribe cops and feed her fellow journalists during late-night deadlines. I also use it in "real life"—to keep the staff of Mysterious Press/Warner Books feeling happy and well-fed!

My secret is using bananas that I've frozen myself. I like to eat them really unripe, so whenever they get a single brown spot I toss them, unpeeled, into the freezer until it's so full I barely have room for my soy bacon and pizza bagels. When it's time for a baking marathon, I thaw them in a sinkful of hot water, snip off the end of the peel, squeeze out the banana like toothpaste, and puree them in the food processor—including all the liquid, which is filled with intense banana flavor. I usually multiply the recipe times eight (no kidding!), which means mixing the batter with a giant spoon in a large lobster pot while standing on a chair. (There's just too much of it for an electric mixer to handle.) Wrapped in plastic and kept in the fridge, it easily stays fresh for more than a week.

> ¾ cup softened butter or margarine
> 1 ¼ cups sugar
> 2 eggs
> 1 ½ cups puréed very ripe bananas
> 1 teaspoon vanilla
> 2 cups flour
> 1 teaspoon baking soda
> 1 teaspoon salt
> ½ cup buttermilk

Cream the butter and sugar together; beat in the eggs, then the bananas and vanilla. In a separate bowl, sift the dry ingredients together. Add alternately with milk to the banana mixture, and make sure everything is mixed evenly.

Put into greased pans: 1 batch fills either 1 9-by-5-by-3-inch pan (generously) or 2 8-by-4-by-2 ½-inch pans (modestly). Make sure to leave ½-inch of space at the top to give the bread room to rise and crown.

Bake at 325 degrees on a single rack for about an hour. Keep checking to make sure the center is cooked but the edges don't burn.

Beth Saulnier's Alex Bernier mysteries feature a twenty-something reporter who solves crimes in her wacky Upstate New York college town. Titles include: *Ecstasy, Bad Seed,* and *Distemper.* Visit www.bethsaulnier.com.

Pinnacle Peak Fry Bread

TWIST PHELAN

Fry bread is a staple made by most of the Native American tribes located in the Southwest, including the Tohono 'O'odham (formerly known as the Papago), the tribe that figures in my Pinnacle Peak mystery series. On my way back from research trips to the reservation, I always stop at a fry bread stand run by an elderly Tohono 'O'odham woman named Anna. While I eat my fill of the warm, delicious treat, Anna tells me about her life as a child on the reservation and Tohono 'O'odham stories, such as how Elder Brother made the 'O'odham, and where rain comes from. The fry bread stand that is a favorite of Hannah Dain, the protagonist of my second book, *Family Claims*, is modeled after Anna's.

4 tablespoons honey
3 tablespoons lard*
1 tablespoon salt
2 cups hot water

1 package active dry yeast
3 cups unbleached white flour
2 teaspoons baking powder
2 to 4 cups additional flour

(*lard is the traditional shortening; vegetable oil may be substituted)

Prepare dough two hours before cooking.

Mix together the honey, lard or vegetable oil, and salt. Stir in the hot water and mix well. Sprinkle the yeast on top of the mixture. Cover with a cloth, and allow to stand about 10 minutes, until the yeast bubbles. Add the flour and baking powder. Stir well. Add more flour (2 to 4 cups) until the dough is firm and cleans hands when mixed. Place the dough in a greased bowl, turning over to grease the top. Cover, and allow to rise until the dough doubles in bulk (about 30 minutes). Punch down and divide in half, then tear each half into eight parts (each ball of dough should be about the size of a peach).

Heat 1 inch or more of lard or vegetable oil to 375 degrees in a frying pan or deep fat fryer. Take a ball of dough, and flatten with your hands, using a stretching action until the dough is very thin and round (about 6 to 8 inches in diameter). Poke a hole in the middle, and drop the dough into the lard or oil. Fry until golden, turning once, about 1 ½ minutes per side.

Remove from the lard or vegetable oil. Drain on paper towels. Top with powdered or cinnamon sugar and honey or jam, and serve immediately.

For a more substantial meal, top the fried dough with your favorite hamburger or taco fixings (shredded beef or chicken, shredded cheese, lettuce, tomato, onion, guacamole, taco sauce, salsa).

Twist Phelan is the author of the Pinnacle Peak mysteries, legal-themed mysteries set in Arizona, each featuring a different sport. Titles include *Heir Apparent* and *Family Claims*. Learn more at www.twistphelan.com

Taryn's Buttermilk Angel Biscuits
SYLVIE KURTZ

On a steamy afternoon when the setting sun bled the raging Red Thunder River red, Texas sheriff Chance Conover forgot who he was. All that filled his mind were muddy images of murder he had to remember before he lost the life he now had.
—from *Remembering Red Thunder*

I took years of ribbing from my husband because my biscuits were never tall and fluffy. I told him it was because I'd never even heard of biscuits until I married him. Then one day, I came across this recipe and—ta, da—no more kidding about flat biscuits! The heroine of this book, Taryn, owns a bakery and these biscuits practically fly off her shelves.

> 2 cups unbleached white flour
> 1 tablespoon sugar
> 1 tablespoon baking powder
> ½ teaspoon salt
> ½ teaspoon baking soda
> ¼ cup vegetable shortening
> 1 package quick-rising yeast
> 1 ¼ cup buttermilk, warmed
> Melted butter (optional)

In a large bowl, sift together the flour, sugar, baking powder, salt, and baking soda. Cut in the shortening until the mixture resembles coarse meal. Add the yeast. Add the warm milk to the dry ingredients, and stir with a fork until moistened. The dough will be sticky.

Turn out the dough onto a heavily floured surface and knead gently until smooth, about 30 seconds. Gently roll out the dough to a ½-inch thickness. Cut with a floured cutter. Arrange the biscuits 2 inches apart on an ungreased baking sheet.

Preheat the oven to 400 degrees while the biscuits rise on the baking sheet, about 15 minutes. Place the biscuits in the oven and bake for 12 to 15 minutes. If desired, brush the tops of the hot biscuits with melted butter.

Makes 12 biscuits.

Sylvie Kurtz is the author of Harlequin Intrigue titles *Remembering Red Thunder* and *Under Lock and Key*. Her website can be found at www.sylviekurtz.com.

A BRUNCH OF CROOKS

Joe Pickett's Mad Scramble Breakfast

CHUCK BOX

$\mathcal{W}$yoming game warden Joe Pickett cooks breakfast for his wife and daughters on weekend mornings, stumbling about the kitchen of his small home in a ratty robe and slippers, always forgetting which burners work and which ones need new elements. While pancakes are generally on the menu, sometimes Joe has time to experiment—like when he's snowed in (*Winterkill*)—and when he knows that if he stays in the kitchen it's much less likely that he'll have to encounter his mother-in-law, who is visiting.

This recipe is an experiment of my own, conducted roughly under the same conditions, although I don't mind seeing my real mother-in-law. The nice thing about the Mad Scramble is that it is good either at home or over a campfire in the Wind River Mountains. Another nice thing about it is that it takes a while to cook, so by the time it's ready everyone is starved and thinks it's better than it is (plus the cook gets some time to read the Sunday paper). My wild game chili is like that also. Oh—don't be put off by the Tater Tots. I've tried real baked potatoes, boiled potatoes, packaged hash browns—and none of them taste as good in the end. Plus, it's rewarding in a perverse way to serve sophisticated people a dish that contains Tater Tots.

1 32-ounce bag frozen Ore-Ida Tater Tots with Onion	6 to 8 eggs
	2 tablespoons minced garlic
1/3 cup olive oil	1/2 green pepper, diced
Seasoned salt	1/4 pound ham, diced or cooked bacon
Pepper	

Pour the thawed Tater Tots into a large skillet with at least half of the olive oil already beginning to smoke at medium-high. As the potatoes cook, break them up into small pieces and turn them often, always adding a little more oil. It should take 20 to 30 minutes for the potatoes to become crisp. Season liberally with seasoned salt and pepper. Don't be shy. While the potatoes cook, break the eggs into a bowl and scramble. Add in the minced garlic, green pepper, and ham or bacon. When the potatoes are golden brown, pour in the egg mixture. Stir the egg mixture to mix thoroughly with the potatoes, constantly turning and chopping with a spatula until the eggs are completely cooked. The green peppers should just be softening. Pour the whole scramble into a serving bowl and serve with thick buttered toast, jalapeño sauce, and ketchup.

Variation: Sometimes, rather than scrambling in the eggs, I add all of the ingredients to the potatoes except the eggs, which I fry or poach on the side. I cover the plate with the potatoes and serve the eggs on top.

Serves 6.

C.J. Box is the winner of the Anthony Award, Macavity Award, Barry Award, and Gumshoe Award, and was a finalist for the Edgar Award and *Los Angeles Times* Book Prize. His Joe Pickett novels include *Open Season*, *Savage Run*, *Winterkill*, and *Wanton Destruction*.

Tomato Gravy On Grits

BILL FITZHUGH

Trying to come up with a recipe that ties in with my books is something of a challenge. Take, for example, *Pest Control*. Now I've eaten fried crickets but I don't have the recipe. I suspect it's something like, 'Catch crickets. Heat oil to 350. Toss the crickets in.' I say that because I don't think a cricket's gonna sit there and let you flour it, drag it through a beaten egg, and then back through the flour. Of course that assumes you want to cook them live, like lobsters or crawfish, maybe that's not the case. I suppose you could knock 'em out with carbon dioxide but, speaking for myself, I don't have any CO_2 in my kitchen. But I digress.

The Organ Grinders provides many more recipe opportunities. The problem is that I detest livers and kidneys and I simply can't bring myself to try hearts or brains. I once wrote a Seinfeld spec script called "The Gourmet Club" wherein Kramer brought prairie oysters (aka swinging beef) to the table but, again, I don't have a tried-and-true recipe, and besides, when was the last time you saw some nice calf testicles at your local market? Now I love sweetbreads (thymus glands!) but they're hard to find and difficult to cook so, maybe next time.

Fender Benders, set in Nashville, features lots of plates of 'fried swimps' but that's too easy. So let's go with something from next year's book, *Radio Activity*. The story is set at a "classic rock" radio station in fictional McRae, Mississippi (my home state). Near the station is a truck stop/diner called Kitty's. My protagonist, Rick Shannon, eats there a lot. They serve all sorts of fine food at this place, including Kitty's Biscuits and her world famous Tater Wads but here is Rick's favorite (and by extension, one of mine): Tomato Gravy on Grits. (This recipe comes from the Jackson, Mississippi Junior League Cookbook, *Come On In*.)

Tomato Gravy

4 tablespoons bacon drippings (or butter if you don't have the bacon fat—in which case, shame on you)
4 tablespoons flour
2 cups milk (heated)
Salt and pepper to taste
1 clove garlic, minced
6 medium tomatoes, seeded and peeled and cut in eighths (or a 28-ounce can) (I grow my own tomatoes and highly recommend you do the same.
Store-boughts are like cooking cotton, but it's your meal, do what you want.)

Melt the drippings in a skillet over medium-high heat. Add the flour and whisk constantly until light brown. Whisk in the warm milk and bring to a boil. Season with salt and pepper, and add the garlic. Reduce the heat, add the tomatoes, and simmer slowly until the tomatoes are soft and integrated into gravy. Serve over grits.

Grits

Don't use instant grits and don't use water!

2 cups milk
⅔ cups grits
1 tablespoon butter
Salt and pepper

Heat the milk over a medium heat, stir in the grits when the milk is warm. Stir frequently until grits are thick and bubbly. Stir in the salt, pepper, and butter. Slap the grits on a plate and ladle tomato gravy over the top. (Note: the milk to grits ratio is always 3:1. 3 cups of milk to 1 cup of grits, or 1 cup of milk to ⅓ cup grits.)

Whatever grits you don't serve you'll want to put in a container and put in the fridge. Fry 'em at your next meal and serve with more tomato gravy.

Bill Fitzhugh writes humorously zany, yet dark mysteries. Titles include *Pest Control* and *Organ Grinders*.

Breakfast with David Dodge
RANDAL BRANDT

David Dodge was born in Berkeley, California on August 18, 1910. His career as a writer began when he made a bet with his wife Elva that he could write a better mystery novel than the one she was reading. He drew on his professional experience as a Certified Public Accountant to create his first series character, San Francisco tax expert and reluctant detective James "Whit" Whitney. *Death and Taxes* was published by in 1941. He won five dollars from Elva. Three more Whitney novels were published between 1943 and 1946.

Dodge went on assignments around the world for *Holiday* and other magazines, and he drew on his travels for material for a series of humorous personal travel journals and as backgrounds for mystery thrillers in exotic locations. His most famous novel is *To Catch a Thief*, set in the French Riviera, which Alfred Hitchcock turned into a film in 1955 starring Grace Kelly and Cary Grant.

This culinary episode occurs in *Bullets for the Bridegroom* (1944) when, a week before he is to report to the army, Whitney and his fiancée, Kitty MacLeod, arrive in Reno to get married and land right into a nest of German spies tracking American ship movements in the Pacific for the Japanese. After driving all night, then having to wait until 9 the next morning to have the "matrimonial welding job" performed, Whit and Kitty spend their "wedding night" at the Truckee Hotel. Pete Weston, an old buddy of Whit's now working with the Associated Press in Nevada, learns of their arrival and meets them at their hotel.

"How about having breakfast with us?"

"Sure. But what about dinner first. It's six o'clock."

"Breakfast," said Whit. "We're night-owls. Where's a good place to eat?"

Pete had to make sure they were really starting the day before he would suggest a restaurant. He had eaten around town so long that he had places picked out for particular meals. When he was convinced that they wanted breakfast and nothing else, he took them down the street to John's Grill.

"It's a Greek joint," he explained on the way. "John's the best fry-cook in town, and he can cook eggs and hamburger like nobody's business, or fried potatoes. But as far as he knows, a green vegetable is something you take out of a can and use for garnish around a steak. Breakfast is fine. Only don't ever order the blue plate dinner."

The Greek joint was small and clean. There was a big range and a steam table between the window and lunch counter, and four or five booths for people who didn't like to sit at the counter. The prop., according to the printed menu, was John Masilikos. He turned out to be cook, as well as prop., and the entire working force of the grill except for one waitress. Pete called him away from the steam table to meet the Whitneys. John was happy to know any friends of Pete. He was a tremendous ape of a man with a close-cropped head, and a bull neck growing from a thicket of black fur on his barrel chest. The black hair covered his forearms and the back of his hands, which were the size and shape of fielder's mitts. He wiped them carefully on his apron before shaking hands with the newlyweds.

"We want the best breakfast you can throw together," Pete said. "Something extra special, John."

John smiled broadly. "Breakfast at six P.M. Try the blue plate dinner."

"I've tried it," Pete said, without enthusiasm. "We want breakfast. Nice thick ham steaks, a lot of eggs, some of those good fried potatoes with onions."

"Ham steaks? Where would I get ham steaks, with meat what it is? I can give you some bacon, maybe."

"Ham steaks," Pete brushed John's objections away. "I know you've got a ham hidden away some place. Do I complain about the Annie Oakley situation when you want to go to the wrestling matches?"

John looked at Kitty and winked. "That's a newspaperman for you. Nothing for nothing. All right, maybe I can find some ham. Go sit down."

He turned back to the range and began rattling frying pans…. The breakfast was all that Pete had led them to expect. John came through generously with the ham, and everything was cooked with the loving touch that a Greek chef gives to things which require frying. Whit and Kitty had not stopped for food since leaving California, so they made up for it until their eyes bulged.

Randal Brandt, a librarian at Bancroft Library at the University of California, Berkeley, created A David Dodge Companion, the official website for mystery and travel writer David Dodge (1910-1974): www.david-dodge.com/.

Jake Diamond's Favorite Hero

(aka Angela Russo's Frittata)
J. L. ABRAMO

*I*n *Catching Water in a Net*, when Los Angeles Crime Boss 'Crazy' Al Pazzo barges into Jake Diamond's San Francisco apartment with his hired muscle in tow—the odds are badly against Jake. Enter Joey Russo to save the day, wielding a potato and egg sandwich wrapped in tin foil hot from his wife's kitchen—leaving it up to Jake to decide which is his favorite hero, Joey or the frittata on seeded Italian bread.

> 4 tablespoons olive oil
> 2 medium potatoes, cut to thinly sliced 1-inch pieces
> 3 scallions, cut to $\frac{1}{4}$-inch lengths
> 1 small red bell pepper, cut in $\frac{1}{2}$-inch strips
> 2 cloves garlic, diced
> 4 eggs, beaten
> Grated Parmesan or Romano cheese (optional)

In a 12-inch skillet (with lid), heat the olive oil. Add the potatoes to the skillet, turning occasionally until they brown. Once the potatoes are brown and crisp, add the peppers and scallions, and continue to sauté until the vegetables are soft. Add the diced garlic and mix well. Spread the potatoes and vegetables uniformly across the bottom of the skillet. Add the beaten eggs (with optional cheese to your taste) uniformly covering the other ingredients. Cover the skillet. When the eggs are browned on the bottom, divide into quarters with a spatula, and turn the 4 segments over. When the second side is browned, plate the frittata.

Serves 4. Can be plated in individual plates or in 1 large serving plate for an authentic Italian free-for-all.

Serving Suggestions:

With toast of your choice (Jake prefers San Francisco sourdough), aka potato, egg, pepper, garlic and scallion Italian omelet.

Wrapped in a tortilla with salsa, aka Frittata fajita.

On fresh Italian or French bread, aka a true Italian hero.

J. L. Abramo is the author of *Catching Water in a Net* and *Clutching at Straws* featuring San Francisco private investigator, Jake Diamond. *Catching Water in a Net* was recipient of the St. Martin's Press/Private Eye Writers of America Award for Best First Private Eye Novel. His website is www.JLABRAMO.com.

Mike Travis' Killer Kona Loco Moco

BARON R. BRITCHER

*L*oco Moco is a true local Hawaiian favorite, and a great cure for a ravenous appetite. When I first moved to Kona, I was introduced to a version of this dish, and have been hooked ever since. This is not the kind of food you'll find at a hotel luau, or as the daily special at Trader Vic's, it is the kind of food you'll eat when asked to join da local boyz for some 'ono grinds' befoa go surf… so go on, geev 'um a try. *Luana Nui!*

> ¾ pound ground beef
> 5 eggs, divided
> 1 package dried onion soup mix
> 2-3 tablespoons shoyu (soy sauce)
> ½ tablespoon cracked pepper
> 1 tablespoon garlic, minced
> Oil (for frying)
> 2 slices white bread, cubed, slightly moistened with water
> ½ cup onion, chopped
> 4 slices white pineapple
> 1 tablespoon butter
> 2 tablespoons flour
> 3 cups water
> 1 tablespoon Worcestershire sauce
> 2 beef bouillon cubes
> 4 cups hot sticky rice

Mix together the ground beef, 1 egg, ½ package of soup mix, shoyu, pepper, minced garlic, and cubes of bread. Shape into 4 patties, and fry in a large skillet until well-browned and cooked to your taste. Remove the patties from the skillet, and set aside to keep warm. Add the chopped onion to the drippings in the skillet, and cook about 5 minutes, until soft. In a separate pan, fry the pineapple slices until light brown in 1 tablespoon butter. Combine the flour with the remaining dry soup mix, and stir into onions. Add water and Worcestershire, and bring to a boil. Crumble bouillon cubes into the skillet, and simmer about 10 minutes, stirring frequently as gravy thickens. Fry the remaining 4 eggs in another skillet, "sunny side up." Place a cup of mounded rice on each of four plates. Top each with a beef patty, pineapple slice and a fried egg. Then smother all with brown gravy and favored condiments of shoyu and catsup.

Serves 4 for breakfast or late night snack!

Mike Travis is the *hapa-haole* protagonist of the hard-boiled novels, *Roadhouse Blues*, *Ruby Tuesday*, and *Run Like Hell*, by author Baron R. Birtcher, of Kona, Hawaii.

Lazy-Cake

MARY SAUMS

My series character, Willi Taft, stays busy with her two careers as both singer in the Nashville music business and fledgling private investigator. In between recording sessions and stake-outs, she has little time for cooking elaborate meals, and opts instead for quick, easy recipes that call for ingredients easily at hand. Her Aunt Sister's Lazy-Cake recipe fits the bill perfectly. This is good for breakfast, or for whipping up when hungry friends stop by unexpectedly.

    ¼ cup butter
    ½ cup all-purpose flour
    ½ cup milk
    2 eggs
    ½ teaspoon nutmeg

In a small iron skillet, melt the butter. Sift the flour into a mixing bowl, and add the milk, stirring just enough to mix. Beat the eggs and add to the flour mixture. Sprinkle nutmeg on top and stir, again just enough to mix. Pour the batter into a hot skillet and bake at 400 degrees for 15 minutes or until light brown.

Maple syrup or confectioner's sugar over strawberry jam can be served on the side, or add your favorite toppings.

Mary Saums' Willi Taft series includes *Midnight Hour*, *The Valley Of Jewels*, and *When The Last Magnolia Weeps*

THE QUICK AND THE DEAD

Ham & Taleggio On Rye

JOHN HARVEY

When I wrote the first Resnick novel, *Lonely Hearts*, some fifteen years ago, one of the things I spent time considering was what—and how—he might eat. This in part because I devote a reasonable (some would say more than reasonable) amount of time thinking about what I might eat—and cook—myself.

And there, straight away, was one of the issues: as a writer, and especially as a writer whose daily stint is often conveniently over by lunchtime, I have both the time—and, thankfully, the inclination—to cook. Charlie, on the other hand, is a busy man, out of the house more often than he is in it, and, the occasional omelette aside, cooking is not what he does. Yet neither is he thin nor undernourished; possessed of a bulky well-fed look, he is not a man to go hungry. Indeed, he is first glimpsed in *Lonely Hearts* with mustard on his tie.

A man, then, who eats but does not linger, a man of appetite. But not, I felt, a man for whom a quick dip into Burger King would suffice. No, I wanted to suggest something beyond the ordinary and pedestrian, something almost exotic in his taste. So, just as a noticeable if aging Polish presence in the city of Nottingham gave me the clue to his ancestry, so the Polish delicatessens in the market where he drank his morning espresso provided the clue to his diet. The salamis, the various kinds of sausage, smoked hams, the differing textures of rye bread....

Fifteen years ago, any sandwich that Resnick fashioned from such ingredients might well have been considered outlandish amongst the general population. Now, with a Pret à Manger in most English town centers offering such daily delights as tandoori salmon and Vietnamese pickle on light rye, or crayfish and rocket with lemon juice and mayonnaise, I suspect Charlie's sandwich concoctions are in danger of seeming humdrum and everyday. But none the less delicious for that. This recipe is adapted from one similar prepared and eaten by Charlie Resnick in the tenth of the series, *Last Rites*.

> Rye bread, not the darkest or densest, possibly with caraway seeds
> 1 thickish slice of smoked ham
> A smallish piece of Taleggio cheese (though not having the same soft texture,
>   Gruyere would be a good substitute)
> A jar of sun-dried tomatoes in oil and/or eggplant similarly preserved
> 1 pickled cucumber (the kind that are ridged and knobbled and the size of a large
>   finger)
> Mustard (Dijon or whole grain)
> Mayonnaise

Cut 2 slices of bread of a good thickness, you don't want the whole thing collapsing about you, and spread each slice with mayonnaise. On 1 slice put several strips of tomato and/or a round of the marinaded eggplant. Trim the fatty edge from the smoked ham (if there's a convenient cat in the vicinity, a trip to the waste bin is saved), and place it on the second slice, smearing it with mustard. Cut away the orange rind from the Taleggio (cue cat), slice the cheese in such a way that it will fit across the ham. Cut the cucumber into thin strips (2 or 4, depending) and place these on top of tomato and/or eggplant. Deftly place this first slice, fenced in as it is by the cucumber, over the other, then, without applying too much pressure, cut in half with a large, sharp knife. Lick your fingers, make sure there are plenty of napkins to hand, and off you go.

Last Rites and *In a True Light* are just two of John Harvey's novels. The John Harvey/Charlie Resnick web site is www.mellotone.co.uk.

The Gunther

ARCHER MAYOR

*I*n this world of gourmet cooks, boutique fooderies, wine bars, 65 coffee flavors, and an obsessive need for fresh oregano, I and my hero, Joe Gunther, occupy a desert island of simple but cloying good taste. So, in honor of his gastronomic fondness for not liking to spend more time cooking than it takes him to eat, Joe Gunther of Vermont would like to offer all of you a tiny but splendid glimpse of practical good taste:

> 2 slices whole wheat bread (for the fiber, natch.)
> Mayonnaise
> Sliced Velveeta
> Jam (be creative here—your choice of flavors. He likes strawberry.)

There you have it! The perfect portable vegetarian meal. Guaranteed to stay with you for several hours. And, hey! Don't knock till you've tried it.

For those of you who haven't met him, Joe Gunther is the lead character in Archer Mayor's Vermont-based series of some 13 police procedurals, including *Tucker Peak*, *The Sniper's Wife*, and *Gatekeeper*.

Glue Hawaii Sandwich

DANIEL KLEIN

When Elvis Presley was in Honolulu for location shots of his seventh film, "Blue Hawaii," he was sidetracked by a local crime spree, the work of the infamous, Grass Skirt Arson. Investigating, Elvis came in contact with a betel nut lady, Lu Hi, who knew of his affection for fried peanut butter and banana sandwiches. In her cunning seduction of Elvis, Hi concocted a variation of this sandwich consisting of a sweet-and-spicy peanut spread and pineapple chunks. It worked like a charm and became one of Elvis' favorites. Dubbed, the Glue Hawaii, it is known for its aphrodisiac effects.

> $\frac{1}{4}$ cup peanut butter
> 1 tablespoon molasses
> 1 teaspoon soy sauce
> 1 teaspoon hot pepper sauce (Tabasco)
> $\frac{1}{4}$ cup canned pineapple chunks
> 2 pieces white bread
> 2 tablespoons butter

In a small bowl, mix the peanut butter, molasses, soy sauce, and hot pepper sauce.

In a separate bowl, mash the pineapple chunks.

Toast the bread lightly. Spread 1 slice of bread with peanut butter mixture, the other slice with the pineapple mash.

Slam the bread together, fry in butter in a medium-hot skillet until brown and mushy.

Slice in half; eat in the presence of a loved one.

Daniel Klein is the author of the Elvis Presley mystery series, *Kill Me Tender, Blue Suede Clues*, and *Viva Las Vengeance*.

Cevapcici

(Grilled Bosnian Meat Sausages with Yogurt Sauce)

DAN FESPERMAN

As a native North Carolinian marooned in Maryland, I can easily sympathize with my Balkan protagonist, Vlado Petric, when he is exiled for years on end in Berlin, far north of his home in Sarajevo, in the early chapters of *The Small Boat of Great Sorrows*. In Maryland, you simply can't get a decent barbecue sandwich, at least not as the treat is defined in the Tar Heel State, where perfection is a hunk of hog, slow-cooked over hickory coals, then chopped and seasoned with cider vinegar and hot pepper flakes. Preferably served with hush puppies. For Vlado, the treat in question is Cevapcici, another meaty delight from the grill, preferably served on pita with onions and a yogurt sauce. Alas, it is virtually unavailable in Berlin except at a few pricey ethnic restaurants. But with a grill and your own ingredients you can at least approximate this Bosnian feast at home. Here's how Vlado likes it prepared, cooked, and served:

1 ½ pounds ground meat (beef, veal, lamb or any combination)
3 cloves garlic, minced   1 ½ teaspoons paprika
½ teaspoon salt   ¼ teaspoon black pepper
Olive oil, for basting (optional)   Pita bread

Mix all the ingredients, except the olive oil and pita, in a large mixing bowl, smushing it together with your hands. Form sausages roughly the same width and half the length of hot dogs, maybe 25 in all. Grill over hot coals (or you may pan fry—no extra grease needed—but only if you're too lazy to do it right!). If you believe it will be too unwieldy dealing with all those sausages, you can place them in a grilling basket (such as you'd use for fish or hot dogs). Flip when they're brown on one side, and repeat, roughly 3 to 4 minutes per side. Baste with the olive oil if needed, but watch for flare-ups. Serve in warmed pockets of pita bread (the fluffier the brand, the better) and top with chopped onions and yogurt sauce. Adding chopped tomatoes and lettuce is okay, too, but this is definitely an Americanization.

Serves 4.

Yogurt sauce

1 pint plain yogurt   ¼ cup peeled, grated cucumber
2 cloves garlic, minced   Juice of half a lemon
Pinch of salt   1 grind of pepper

Mix all the ingredients.

Dan Fesperman is the author of two Vlado Petric novels—*Lie in the Dark*, which won the British Crime Writers Association's John Creasey Memorial Dagger Award for best first novel, and *The Small Boat of Great Sorrows*. He is completing his third book, *The Fixer of Peshawar*, a suspense novel set in Pakistan and Afghanistan.

Cassie Burdette's Company Hot Dog Casserole
ROBERTA ISLEIB

*C*assandra Burdette, the aspiring professional golfer in my golf mystery series, has so far shown no signs of talent in the kitchen. (Cassie informs me, in snooty tones, that it's hard to cook when you're always on the road.) If takeout isn't available, she suggests this easy dish.

    1 medium onion, chopped
    1 small green pepper, chopped
    Olive oil
    6 to 8 best quality hot dogs, sliced into rounds
    1 very large can B&M baked beans
    2 tablespoons Dijon mustard
    3 tablespoons barbeque sauce
    2 tablespoons molasses or brown sugar
    Worcestershire sauce

Sauté the onions and peppers in a small amount of olive oil. Set aside.

Sauté the hot dog slices until brown. Mix these ingredients with the baked beans, pork fat removed and discarded. Add the mustard, barbeque sauce, molasses or brown sugar, and Worcestershire sauce to taste. Mix and pour into a greased 9-by-11-inch casserole. Bake at 350 until bubbly.

Roberta Isleib's has written *Six Strokes Under*, *A Buried Lie*, and *Board to Death*. Visit her website at www.robertaisleib.com.

Dash's Favorite Meal
CAROL LEA BENJAMIN

Everyone in New York has a kitchen drawer full of take-out menus. But don't look there for the pizzeria number. It's on speed dial. Not only that, you probably know it by heart.

Here's Rachel Alexander and Dash's favorite meal:

1. Order a pie from your local pizzeria.
2. Set aside three slices to cool for your dog.
3. Your dog's slices will be ready to serve when you are halfway through your own.

Carol Lea Benjamin

Carol Lea Benjamin is the Shamus Award-winning author of the Rachel Alexander and Dash mysteries, including *This Dog for Hire* and *The Long Good Boy*, as well as eight best-selling dog training books. She can be reached via her website: www.CarolLeaBenjamin.com.

Don't Forget Your Best Friend
PATRICIA GUIVER

Dog biscuits are often featured in my Delilah Doolittle, Pet Detective series. Delilah usually has a supply on hand to lure, calm, distract, or reward the canines that cross her path. A particular favorite of Watson, Delilah's Doberman sidekick, are Peanut Butter Oatmeal Biscuits. The recipe is borrowed, with permission, from *Cooking with Calhoune*, published by Basset Hound Rescue of Southern California.

Watson's Favorite Peanut Butter Oatmeal Dog Biscuits

4 cups whole wheat flour
2 cups oatmeal
½ to ¾ cup peanut butter
2 ½ cups hot water

Preheat oven to 350 degrees. Mix all the ingredients together, adding more hot water if the dough is too stiff. Roll out the dough on a floured board to ¼ inch thick. Cut with a bone-shaped cookie cutter. Place 1 inch apart on greased cookie sheets. Bake until brown and crisp, about 30 minutes.

Note: Biscuits should be refrigerated or frozen for long-term storage.

Makes approximately 6 dozen. The recipe can be halved.

Patricia Guiver writes the Delilah Doolittle Pet Detective mysteries, which include *The Beastly Bloodline, Delilah Doolittle and the Missing Macaw,* and *Delilah Doolittle and the Canine Chorus.*

Dad's Pizza

TOM MITCHELTREE

*T*his has been a favorite of my kids for years, and I've always noticed that a few extra of their friends show up when I make it. I consider this pizza to be slow death by high cholesterol. The best thing about it is that even people who do not like you will ask for seconds.

Dough

2 ½ cups all-purpose flour
1 package rapid-rising dry yeast
½ teaspoon salt

⅔ cup very warm water
1 tablespoon honey
1 tablespoon olive oil

Mix the dry ingredients in a large bowl. Add the honey and olive oil to the warm water and mix. Add the wet and dry ingredients together, mix, and then knead into a ball. Leave the ball in bowl, covered, and let rise at room temperature.

This is enough dough to make 2 12-inch round pizza crusts.

Toppings

1 pound ground beef
Olive oil
1 jar tomato sauce (we like the onion/garlic mix the best)
1 package small, round, thin Canadian bacon slices
1 can pineapple bits
1 pound mozzarella cheese
1 package, small, round, thin pepperoni slices
1 package sliced mushrooms
1 small can sliced olive

Brown the hamburger and break it up into small bits. Divide the dough in half and make 2 round pizza crusts. In the center of each crust, pour a small pool of olive oil and then about ⅓ jar of sauce. Spread to cover the crust. Layer both pizzas with the hamburger bits. On top of one pizza, cover the hamburger with Canadian bacon rounds, liberally sprinkle with pineapple bits, and then cover completely with grated mozzarella cheese.

For the second pizza, cover the hamburger with pepperoni rounds, liberally add mushroom slices and sliced olive bits, and then cover completely with grated mozzarella cheese.

Bake both pizzas together at 400 degrees for approximately 12 to 15 minutes, or until the cheese is melted and the edges of the crusts are browned.

The combination of the honey, olive oil, and ground beef gives this pizza a unique flavor and a rich texture.

Tom Mitcheltree's mysteries include *Katie's Will*, *Katie's Gold*, *Blink of an Eye*, and *Terror in Room 201*.

Jesse Ascencio's Cultural Assimilation Cheeseburger
KENT BRAITHWAITE

Jesse Ascencio, my Southern California private eye, is a contemporary PI operating in the storied SoCal venue of Philip Marlowe, Lew Archer, and Kinsey Millhone. The turf has been well traveled by countless sleuths throughout the history of mystery fiction, yet I made Jesse representative of Southern California in our new millennium by having him be the grandson of Mexican immigrants who moved to this country without the benefits of official documents. While Jesse is proud of his Hispanic heritage, cultural assimilation is the overarching theme of my series.

This assimilation theme is perhaps best represented in the debut novel of the series, *The Wonderland Murders*, when Jesse wines and dines an attractive woman, an employee of county government, hoping she'll provide him with information crucial to his multiple-murder investigation. As the waitress arrives at their table, Jesse orders a custom designed cheeseburger that includes the restaurant's largest beef patty topped with American cheese between a whole-wheat roll, and loaded with lettuce, tomatoes, pickles, onions, bacon, guacamole, and a touch of salsa. He states that the burger reminds him of himself, but the guacamole, properly prepared, is crucial to the taste of Jesse's All-American and culturally-assimilated sandwich.

When he is home with time to cook, Jesse's guacamole recipe runs as follows:

Peel an avocado and remove the seed. Cut the avocado into small pieces; place it in a bowl and mash.

Chop a tomato into small pieces. Add the chopped tomato, some lemon juice, garlic salt, pepper, cilantro, and onions to taste. Chopped chiles may be added if additional spice is desired.

Chill for at least an hour in the refrigerator. Serve chilled as a dip for chips, a topping for Jesse Ascencio's Cultural Assimilation Cheeseburger, or your own mysterious concoction.

Kent Braithwaite is the author of the Jesse Ascencio PI novel series, which includes *The Wonderland Murders,* as well as the Casey McGraw Bush League Baseball Mystery short stories.

Cody O'Brien's Root-Party Float

DANIELLE GIRARD

*L*ike their creator, the protagonists of my novels can't cook to save their lives. I recently bought a crock pot, thinking the perfect cooking for me is to create something and leave it for eight hours, come back, and voila dinner! Warning: don't put rice in the crock pot for eight hours. I told my husband it was cous cous, but I don't think he bought it.

> *Rookie cop Alex Kincaid hunted through the kitchen for something to eat. She found a box of penne then checked the refrigerator for pasta sauce. Besides the milk, of which she polished off almost a gallon a week, there was little else in the refrigerator. She had tried to keep vegetables, but even carrots couldn't survive long enough for her to get around to eating them."*

—from *Ruthless Game*

But, ex-FBI computer intrusion Squad Agent Cody O'Brien (from *Cold Silence*) is a single mom, so she is the most established of the cooks in my books. On the run from the FBI, she and her son, R.J., throw a regular "root" party where they dye their hair dark and eat things with "root."

> *"Mom?" R.J. said after a regular tickle match.*
> *Cody looked up. "Yeah?"*
> *He crossed his arms. "You've got roots."*
> *Cody sat up and looked at her son's dark hair. They were light-haired naturally, but she and R.J. had been dying their hair since they'd left New Orleans. "Guess it's time for a root party."*
> *"Can we have root beer floats?"*
> *"Of course. And beet roots."*
> *R.J. scrunched his nose. "The beet roots were gross, Mom."*
> *"Okay, we'll stick with floats."*

1 can Dad's root beer
2 scoops (about $\frac{3}{4}$ cup) vanilla ice cream (nothing fat-free or low-fat, please!)

Pour half of the root beer into a 16-ounce soda glass and spoon ice cream into glass. Top with the remaining root beer.

Yields about 2 cups.

Danielle Girard is the author of *Savage Art, Ruthless Game, Chasing Darkness,* and *Cold Silence.* Visit her at www.daniellegirard.com.

Hot Fudge Sauce

ELIZABETH J. MORRIS

$\mathcal{M}$argaret Anne Philips, my series protagonist, is known for her Hot Fudge Sauce, which she makes for Christmas every year and gives as gifts to friends. She also makes it on and off throughout the year for herself and for friends:

> *When she finally climbed the stairs to her condominium, she wondered idly what she would fix for dinner. Dan was asleep when she got to their apartment, so she went into the kitchen to check the fridge, deciding on ham sandwiches and mushroom soup with ice cream and Pepperidge Farm cookies. She would save her homemade fudge sauce to take to Shiranda's next weekend.*

> 2 sticks butter
> 2 cups granulated sugar
> 4 to 5 ounces unsweetened cocoa
> 2 cans unsweetened canned milk
> Pinch of salt
> Vanilla

Melt the butter in a large pan. Add the granulated sugar, cocoa, milk, and salt. Stir constantly with a whisk over a medium heat until it thickens. Add a good dollop of vanilla, then spoon into glass containers. This is a very forgiving recipe, a little more butter is fine, a little whipping cream would be fine, more or less cocoa to taste is fine: darker, more, lighter, less. As my mystery writer friend Philip Craig would say: "Delish."

Elizabeth J. Morris has written a series of five mysteries, including *An Elusive Inheritance*, *An Elusive Revenge*, and *An Unlikely Treasure*.

A CRIMINAL PAST-A

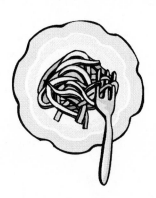

Rigatoni Putenesca

ELIZABETH GEORGE

A word of warning: Everyone who has an Italian mother knows that good Italian cooking is dependent upon measuring nothing. *A bit of this* and *a handful of that* tend to be the measurements one uses when preparing anything from that part of the world. Thus, I am able only to approximate the quantities of ingredients required for this tasty dish. It is, by the way, reputed to be the dish made by Italian prostitutes while waiting between clients. Hence, the name. It's fast, delicious, and a definite crowd pleaser. The only time I had trouble with it was when I inadvertently served it to a woman with a deadly allergy to anything with fins. Oh well. She passed on with a smile.

> Olive oil
> 1 or 2 cloves garlic
> 1 large onion
> Salt and pepper
> Parsley
> 1 quart of Aunt Nene's fresh canned tomatoes (if you don't have an Aunt Nene
>   with a garden, you can make do with 1 large can of diced tomatoes. For every
>   two people you plan to serve, you need 1 quart of Aunt Nene's tomatoes or 1
>   large can of anyone else's.)
> 1 tin anchovies in olive oil
> 1 can kalamata olives
> 1 jar capers
> Fresh basil
> Fresh, imported Pecorino Romano cheese (accept no substitute)
> 1 package rigatoni

Get a nice big pot out of your cupboard and cover the bottom of it with olive oil. How much, you ask? Haven't a clue. Remember, this is Italian cooking we're talking about. I cover the bottom with about $\frac{1}{8}$- to $\frac{1}{4}$-inch of olive oil. Heat it up for a minute or so. Medium or high. Doesn't make much difference.

Peel the cloves of garlic (always a good idea) and brown them in the olive oil. They should be nicely brown but not burnt. If they burn, you have to throw them out and start with new oil because 1) Aunt Nene will haunt you if you don't and 2) the olive oil will taste bitter.

Add the onion, which I hope you've had the good sense to chop first. Chop it up nice and coarse, because no Italian cook worth her salt chops onions neatly. This should be a cheap brown onion, by the way. No fancy pants stuff or you'll wreck the recipe.

Add some salt and fresh ground pepper. Not too much salt. Be careful because of the anchovies to come.

Add a whole lot of parsley. How much, you ask? Well, I throw in a handful and I wear size seven gloves. Figure it out. I mostly eyeball it. If it doesn't look like I have enough, I throw in more. Remember, if you use fresh parsley, you have to make sure it's Italian parsley and not that disgusting stuff they use to decorate dinner dishes in cheap restaurants. That tastes like the tops of old pantyhose, anyway. (Don't ask.) Also, if you use fresh parsley, you have to use a whole bunch more and I don't know how much because I never use fresh parsley.

Stir it all up for a minute or so, then add the tomatoes. Stir them up. Sing a verse of *Volare* by Bobby Rydell. (Surely you remember him, don't you? If not, something by Frank Sinatra will do.)

Drain most of the olive oil from the anchovies and dump them into the tomato mixture. They will cook down to nothing and just be the background flavor of this sauce.

Let all of this simmer for about 25 minutes...although in a pinch you could probably get away with 15.

While it's simmering, pit a slew of kalamata olives. The easiest way to do this is to squish them individually with the back of a spoon, which will split them. Then just pluck out the pit. How many olives is a slew, you ask? No clue. Maybe twenty?

Drain all of the liquid from the capers.

Now, if you haven't thought about it by now, for heaven's sake start the water for the rigatoni. If I have to tell you how to cook it, you'd better not even try this recipe. Go out to dinner instead. Anyway, if you know how to cook it, you know to cook it *al dente*, which means that it's chewy. If it's moosh-a-moosh, as my mother used to say, it will be terrible. Life will be terrible. You will want to jump from the nearest bridge.

As the rigatoni approaches perfection, (like about one minute from that point), dump the capers into the tomato sauce. Stir for 30 seconds or so. Follow this up with the kalamata olives.

Now you've got to be fast because if the olives are in the sauce too long, you've got a major taste problem on your hands.

Drain the rigatoni when it's done. Top it with the sauce. Over each individual serving, grate a very nice amount of the Pecorino Romano cheese. Follow up with a healthy sprinkling of fresh basil.

Serve with Aunt Nene's broccoli. (Don't know how to prepare it? Darn!)

At any rate, enjoy.

Elizabeth George has published more than a dozen books, including *A Place of Hiding* and the short story collection *I, Richard*. Her Inspector Lynley mysteries include *Payment in Blood* and *In Pursuit of the Proper Sinner*. Her work has won the Anthony and Agatha Awards and France's *Le Grand Prix de Literature Policiere*, and has also been nominated for the Edgar and the Macavity Awards. You can contact her through her website at www.elizabethgeorgeonline.com.

George's Spaghetti Sauce
GEORGE PELECANOS

When I am writing a book I work odd hours, so when dinnertime comes around our meals have to be prepared on the fly. I make enough of the following spaghetti sauce to last two or three weeks. My wife is a vegetarian, so this doesn't work for her, but my sons and daughter love it. In fact, young folks from all over the neighborhood mysteriously show up for dinner on those nights that Mr. P's sauce is being served. That's cool with me; I love to see kids get down on their food. Don't cheat on this recipe. It doesn't work unless it's cooked for four hours. The pork chop should be dropped whole, on the bone, into the mix. The cooking time will allow it to "fall apart." Enjoy.

>   3 onions, chopped
>   Olive oil
>   2 cloves garlic, finely chopped
>   ½ green pepper, chopped
>   1 pound ground beef
>   1 pork chop, bone in
>   2 large cans tomato paste
>   3 large cans tomato sauce
>   4 large cans water
>   3 bay leaves
>   Salt and pepper to taste

Sauté the chopped onions in hot olive oil. Add the garlic and green pepper. Add the ground beef. Stir until brown. Add 1 bone-in pork chop. Add the tomato paste, tomato sauce, and water. Add bay leaves and salt and pepper to taste. Stir and simmer for 4 hours.

Note: The pork chop is key.

George Pelecanos is an award-winning journalist, screenwriter, independent film producer, and the author of eleven highly-regarded crime novels set in and around Washington, D.C., including *Right as Rain, Hell to Pay,* and *Soul Circus.*

Killer Spaghetti Sauce
LESLIE O'KANE

This recipe is my personal favorite of all my mother's recipes, though I modified it to reflect my own tastes, much to Mom's annoyance. My sleuths don't tend to be especially good cooks.

1 small container (6-ounce) dried mushrooms
   (optional if you have finicky children, but they're delicious in this recipe—
   the mushrooms, not your children)
1 pound ground beef
½ bunch green onions, chopped (or 1 finely chopped medium onion,
   if you want to side with my mother)
2 cloves of garlic (or just 1, again, if you're Mom)
2 teaspoons basil
Dash of salt and pepper
1 large can (28-ounce) Progresso Italian plum tomatoes
   (or 2 16-ounce cans cheaper-but-not-as-tasty {trust me!} tomatoes)
2 cans Campbell's beef consommé

Soak the mushrooms for 30 minutes, then drain. In a Dutch oven, fry the beef. Add the onions and minced garlic, and continue cooking until the meat is well done. Add the seasoning and mushrooms.

Add the tomatoes and chop them with a spoon into 3 or 4 pieces per tomato. Add the beef soup. Simmer, stirring occasionally, for 1 hour.

Serve over 16 ounces of spaghetti, cooked according to the package directions.

Serves 4 to 5.

Leslie O'Kane's Molly Masters series includes *Death of a PTA Goddess* and her Allie Babcock series includes *Give the Dog a Bone*. She is working on a third series.

Munch Mancini's Meatballs

BARBARA SERANELLA

*A*fter a tough week of fixing cars and catching bad guys, Munch Mancini sometimes cooks. One of her specialties is her delicious meatballs. She first made these when she was a teenager and hanging out with bikers. Now she makes them for friends and family, and they get better when they've sat overnight in the refrigerator and are warmed up the next day.

    1 pound ground beef
    ½ pound pork or Italian sausage
    1 cup Contadina bread crumbs
    2 eggs
    ½ cup chopped onion
    3 cloves garlic, minced
    Milk as needed for consistency (the mixture should be tacky and must stick together)
    Olive oil

Mush all the ingredients except the oil together with your hands, and form golf ball-size meatballs. Fry them in medium hot olive oil until browned, then carefully drop them into a pot of simmering marinara sauce, and cook for hours, filling the house with the scent.

The Marinara Sauce

    Olive oil
    ½ onion, chopped
    3 garlic cloves
    3 8-ounce cans of chopped tomatoes
    1 small can of mushrooms
    Basil, oregano, garlic, pepper, salt, bay leaf, and a touch of cloves
    Red wine

Pour olive oil, covering the bottom of a large sauce pan (I use a Dutch oven) until it glistens. Sauté the onion and garlic until transparent. Add the tomatoes, mushrooms, liberal shakes of all the spices, and several chugs of the wine. (Munch had to wait until she was 15-years-sober and involved with a guy who drank alcohol before bottles of open wine could be found in her kitchen. The alcohol cooks out.)

Bring the mixture to a boil and then reduce heat. Cook as long as possible. Tomato sauce cannot be overcooked.

Serve over pasta with grated fresh imported Regianno Parmesan cheese.

Barabara Seranella's lively Munch Mancini crime novel series includes *Unpaid Dues, Unfinished Business* and *No Man Standing*. Pay Munch a visit at www.barbaraseranella.com.

Joanna's Chicken Stuffed Pasta Shells

ELEANOR TAYLOR BLAND

My grandson, Anthony wants to be a chef and is a very good cook, coming up with his own recipes. Not only does he create recipes by Joanna for my books, but he is also working with a cookbook author to develop recipes for people who are allergic to everything! Five or six of his recipes will be in a booklet for me to give away when I go to Bouchercon.

And, at 15, he is also an author…we co-authored "Murder on the Southwest Chief," which will be in the anthology *Shades of Black: Mystery Fiction by African American Authors* for which I am the editor.

Here's one of his recipes:

    1 medium onion
    4 cloves garlic or to taste
    ½ pound sliced mushrooms
    ⅔ cup olive oil
    1 large can tomato puree
    1 can diced tomatoes or fresh diced tomatoes, if desired
    Seasoning to taste
    1 box large pasta shells
    4 cups diced cooked chicken breasts
    ½ cup Parmesan cheese
    ½ cup Romano cheese

Sauté the onions, garlic, and mushrooms in the olive oil. Add the tomato puree and tomatoes. Simmer 20 minutes. Season to taste.

Cook the large shells. Mix the chicken with the cheeses. Stuff the shells with the chicken mixture.

Pour half of the sauce into a shallow baking dish and add the stuffed shells. Pour the remaining sauce over the shells.

Cover with foil. Bake at 350 degrees for 35 to 40 minutes.

Eleanor Taylor Bland's mysteries, featuring African-American police detective Marti Macalister, include *Dead Time*, *Tell No Tales*, and *Whispers in the Dark*.

Mom's Lasagna
VICTORIA THOMPSON

My mother's lasagna was legendary. Whenever she served it, people wanted the recipe. Whenever I made it, people wanted the recipe. For many years, I prided myself on making authentic Italian lasagna because the recipe had come from my father's Italian family, but a few years ago, I discovered that the recipe had actually come from my Dad's cousin's non-Italian wife to my non-Italian mother and wasn't authentic Italian at all. It still gets rave reviews, though. I chose it for this collection because my latest book, *Murder on Mulberry Bend*, features Italian immigrants living in the Lower East Side of Manhattan in turn-of-the-century New York, and is dedicated to my authentic Italian grandparents.

Sauce

    2 pounds ground beef
    1 12-ounce can of tomato paste
    1 40-ounce can tomato puree
    4 cloves garlic, minced
    1 tablespoon salt
    ½ teaspoon pepper
    1 teaspoon oregano

Brown the ground beef and drain the fat. Combine with the other ingredients, and simmer for at least 20 minutes. Layer in a 9-by-12-inch pan with:

    Lasagna noodles, cooked as directed
    1 pound Mozzarella cheese, shredded or grated
    ½ pound Ricotta cheese, shredded or grated
    1 cup Parmesan cheese, shredded or grated

Layer as follows: noodles, ⅓ of sauce, half of cheeses, noodles, ⅓ of sauce, half of cheese, sauce. Sprinkle Parmesan cheese on top.

Bake at 375 degrees for 20 minutes, or until the sauce bubbles around the edges and the cheeses are thoroughly melted. May be prepared ahead of time and be refrigerated or frozen for future use. Reheated leftovers taste even better.

Victoria Thompson's Gaslight Mystery series, which features midwife Sarah Brandt and police detective Frank Malloy, includes *Murder on Washington Square*, *Murder on Gramercy Park*, and the Edgar-nominated *Murder on St. Mark's Place*. Visit her at www.victoriathompson.com.

Pasta with Porcini Mushrooms

ED GOLDBERG

I try to have my PI, Lenny Schneider, cook at least one meal in each book. Of the many things we have in common (beer, baseball, jazz, food), cooking brings us closest together. Living well is the best revenge, and good cooking is a big part of it.

1 ounce dried Porcini mushrooms
1-pound can of Italian-style (Roma) tomatoes
2 to 3 smoked pork chops, or ½ pound of good smoked ham
4 to 5 large shallots, or 1 medium onion plus 3 cloves of garlic
2 tablespoons good quality virgin olive oil
1 teaspoon dried parsley, or 1 tablespoon fresh
A few twists of fresh-ground black pepper
A dash or 2 of cayenne (optional)
1 teaspoon dried basil, or 1 tablespoon fresh
1 cup chicken broth or consomme
½ cup of white wine, preferably dry vermouth
2 to 3 tablespoons tomato paste (optional)
12 ounces of fresh linguini or fettucine, cooked *al dente*

Lightly rinse the sand off of the dried Porcinis with cold water. Soak them for 15 minutes in enough boiling water to make 1 ½ cups of mushrooms and water.

Chop the tomatoes, reserving the liquid left in the can. Cut the pork chops or ham into small strips or chunks. Mince the shallots or onion/garlic. When the mushrooms are soft, cut the bigger pieces and the tougher stems into smaller pieces. Reserve the soaking liquid.

In a saucepan or skillet, sauté the shallots or onion/garlic, in the olive oil until translucent. Do not burn. Add the pork or ham and stir-fry for a minute. Add the tomatoes, mushrooms, pepper, cayenne (if desired), parsley, and basil, and bring slowly to a simmer. Simmer for about 10 minutes, add the broth, wine, the balance of tomato juice, and about ¼ cup of the mushroom liquid. Avoid the sand at the bottom.

Simmer, covered, for about a half an hour, until the tomatoes have softened. Add the mushroom liquid if needed. You may add some tomato paste (2 to 3 tablespoons), stirred in while the sauce is simmering, if the sauce seems too thin, but it will change the flavor.

Prepare the pasta so that it finishes about the same time as the sauce. Toss the well-drained pasta with the sauce. If desired, sprinkle on fresh-grated Romano or Pecorino cheese.

Ed Goldberg is the author of two Lenny Schneider mysteries, *Served Cold*, which won the Shamus Award in 1995, and *Dead Air*.

Serena's Spinach & Pasta
NATALIE BUSKE THOMAS

I write the "pizza detective" Serena Wilcox mystery series. The pizza nickname emerged when readers noticed that Serena, my private detective character, eats a lot of pizza and junk food. Readers sent me pizza toys, web pages, and recipes. I loved the pizza tie-in to my books! But all of this changed when I wanted to get pregnant. A year of negative pregnancy tests, infertility treatments, and emotional chaos ended with a diagnoses of insulin resistance. I was instructed to follow a diabetic diet and exercise plan to get my blood sugar under control. No more pizza buffets!

Happily I was pregnant two months after starting my fitness plan. I felt great! Unfortunately I developed gestational diabetes during the pregnancy and had a horrendously long nine months. Joyously our baby girl was born healthy and beautiful the week before Christmas 2001. Now I'm a reformed junk food junkie. Although I still indulge—I'm a work in progress—my new fitness lifestyle affects every area of my life. In my writing, I'll be pushing changes onto Serena Wilcox (will she accept this gracefully?). I doubt she'll ever shed her "pizza detective" alias, but her surprising talent as a gourmet cook will be revealed in my next mystery, *Shed Secrets*.

Serena's Spinach & Pasta is healthy but tastes good; easy but looks impressive! (Take a picture of this one, it'll make you look like a gourmet cook!)

As a Side Dish

1 tablespoon or so olive oil
1 package frozen chopped spinach
1 small box "bow ties" pasta (12 ounces)
1 can cream of chicken soup
Parmesan cheese

Use your favorite nonstick skillet (the deeper variety). Heat the olive oil. Add the frozen chopped spinach. When the spinach has broken apart (but not cooked yet), dump in the "bow ties" pasta. Stir in the cream of chicken soup. Sprinkle some Parmesan cheese over the whole thing, stir. Stir occasionally until the pasta is tender. This recipe is very flexible. Add water if you want to thin it down, flavor it up with black pepper or garlic.

This makes an impressive side dish. I served it to some new friends—our guests had second helpings!

As a Main Dish

1 tablespoon or so olive oil
Chicken strips (about ¾ to 1 pound)
1 16-ounce bag frozen broccoli "stir fry" vegetables
1 package frozen chopped spinach
1 16-ounce box of rice *or* 1 12-ounce box pasta
1 can chicken broth
1 can cream of mushroom soup
Parmesan cheese

Again, use your favorite deep nonstick skillet. Need that olive oil (use just enough to lightly coat, no drowning!) Brown some chicken strips (you can make the pieces bite size if you wish). Add the frozen broccoli "stir fry" vegetables and frozen chopped spinach. Add either rice or pasta (rotini works well). Pour in a can of chicken broth. Stir in a can of cream of mushroom soup. Top with Parmesan cheese and mix well.

Cover. When the pasta and vegetables are tender to your liking, your well-rounded healthy meal is complete! And it tastes creamy—"comfort food." This is a dish (and variations of it…I throw together what I happen to have in my cupboard) that I make often for my family.

Natalie Buske Thomas writes the fun and suspenseful Serena Wilcox Mysteries, which includes *Virtual Memories, Camp Conviction,* and *Shed Secrets.* You can visit her at www.independentmysteries.com.

Deadline Dinner
LESLIE O'GRADY

When I'm facing a deadline and have little time to cook, I rely on this family favorite. The casserole is easy to prepare, tastes great the next day, and individual portions may be frozen.

    ¾ pound elbow macaroni
    1 pound ground sirloin
    1 tablespoon olive oil
    1 clove garlic, minced
    1 large white onion, chopped
    1 cup sliced white mushrooms
    2 large green peppers, cored, seeded, and chopped
    1 teaspoon oregano or Italian seasoning
    1 ½ jars (26-ounce size) spaghetti sauce
    1 cup mozzarella cheese, shredded or grated

Boil the macaroni until al dente, and drain.

Brown the sirloin in a large nonstick pan. When browned, remove and set aside. In the same pan, heat the olive oil, and add the garlic. Add the onions, and cook until translucent. Add the mushrooms and peppers, sautéing until tender. Return the sirloin to the pan. Add the sauce and spices. Simmer for 5 to 10 minutes. Add the macaroni and stir. Pour into a large casserole dish and top with the mozzarella.

Bake in a 350-degree oven until the cheese melts. Serve with a tossed salad and garlic bread. Refrigerate leftovers for the following day, or freeze individual portions for another deadline.

Serves 4.

The Grateful Undead is the first in Leslie O'Grady's humorous contemporary mystery series featuring Wanda Miranda LaFortuna, former actress and private investigator's assistant.

RED HERRINGS

Bachelor Salmon
JEREMIAH HEALY

One of the many advantages of being a full-time writer is that you can work wherever you can plug in your computer and modem. As a result, I've been privileged to spend January through April in South Florida for the last six years, even setting two of the John Cuddy private-investigator mysteries, *Rescue* and *Spiral,* in the Keys and in Fort Lauderdale, respectively. However, my wife (who has, she likes to remind me, a "real" job back in Boston) can join me for only a part of each season, and I'm not much on cooking (or cleaning) myself (basically, if you can't Shake 'N Bake it, I don't make it). I have found, though, that the following recipe is a terrific bachelor/bachelorette meal: Simple, tasty, and healthy.

Buy a ½ pound of salmon filet, with a thicker piece better than a thin or irregular one. 30 minutes before cooking, remove it from the fridge. Take a regular dinner plate that's microwave safe, and spray some Pam on the eating surface. Then slide the filet, scales side *down,* onto the plate.

Using a marinade you like, first poke holes with a fork into the salmon flesh, then pour on a little marinade, then poke holes again *through* the marinade, then spread the marinade with the edge of the fork so it's fairly even. Leave the salmon at room temperature, but put a piece of plastic over it *lightly* (flies before, and splatter during, cooking). *Do not use this marinade fork again unless you clean it thoroughly.*

During the half-an-hour, make a nice salad, open a bottle of wine, and pre-ossify yourself with a glass or two.

When all is ready, put the salmon plate with plastic overlay into the microwave, set the timer to 4 or 5 minutes on high (assuming you have a rotating oven; if not, just turn the plate every minute or so). Do *not* flip the filet over at any time.

When the binger says the fish is done, use an oven mitt to draw the plate out. Throw the plastic overlay into the sink (*not* the trash: it'll be too hot). Set the plate down where you intend to eat it, but put a trivet or placemat down first in deference to the furniture finish.

I usually zap some frozen hunk bread to go with this, though the overall beauty of this meal from a solo-chef/diner standpoint is that you've used just one plate (for both cooking and eating), one salad bowl, two forks, one knife, and one wineglass to get a very fast, minimal clean-up refueling. Enjoy.

Jeremiah Healy is the current president of the International Association of Crime Writers and, under the pseudonym Terry Devane is also the author of the Mairead O'Clare Boston-based legal-thriller series, which includes *Uncommon Justice, Juror Number Eleven,* and *A Stain Upon the Robe.*

Brady Coyne's Poached Trout
WILLIAM G. TAPPLY

A poacher is someone who catches fish illegally. That's not what we mean.... Brady Coyne is a Boston lawyer who'd rather fly-fish for trout than accrue billable hours. He's gone fishing at one time or another in all twenty of his novels, and he's discovered that fooling wild trout requires many of the same deductive skills as solving murders. Brady puts back most of the fish he catches. But now and then he honors a special guest with a trout dinner. Wild trout, cooked within an hour after they're caught, are incomparable. His favorite way to cook trout is to poach them in butter, olive oil, wine, and rosemary. Cooked this way, the flesh is moist and tasty, and falls away from the skeleton, so that fish bones don't interfere with the eating.

> 4 freshly-caught trout, 8 to 12 inches long
> Salt and fresh-ground pepper
> 1 tablespoon virgin olive oil
> 1 golf-ball-size glob butter
> ¼ cup white cooking wine
> Dash of rosemary

Prepare the fish by slitting open the body cavity and removing the innards and gills. Cut off the heads. Wash thoroughly in cold water, and pat dry with a paper towel. Sprinkle the cavity with salt and freshly ground pepper. Heat the olive oil and butter in a 12-inch skillet. When the butter has melted, add the wine and a generous dash of rosemary. Lay the trout on their sides and cover the skillet. Cook 3 minutes, then turn the fish over and cook for another 3 minutes. Serve immediately and ceremoniously, 2 trout per person, with wild rice, a seasonal green vegetable (Brady prefers asparagus), fresh garden greens, a suitably expensive white wine, and a Miles Davis CD.

Brady Coyne has narrated all twenty of William G. Tapply's mysteries, including *a Fine Line* and most recently, *Shadow of Death*. Tapply has also published nine books, and hundreds of stories, essays, and articles about fishing and the outdoors.

Jessica Fletcher's Maine Lobster Pie

JESSICA FLETCHER AND DONALD BAIN

*D*own East, we like a hearty winter meal. This lobster pie—or stew, if you use more cream and less thickening—works as well with fresh lobster or leftover lobster (a rarity in my kitchen, given my friend Dr. Seth Hazlitt's appetite) or frozen lobster. Warning: It isn't low-calorie or low-cholesterol, but it is a delicious and flexible recipe.

> 1 pound cooked lobster meat, cut up
> 5 tablespoons butter, melted (and divided)
> $\frac{1}{4}$ cup sherry or Madeira
> 1 tablespoon flour
> 1 cup light cream or half-and-half
> 2 egg yolks (or 3 to 4 slices of white bread, crusts removed, and torn into pieces)
> Seasonings to taste*
> Topping**

Sauté the lobster lightly in 2 tablespoons of melted butter, and sprinkle with sherry. Cook till the alcohol evaporates (don't overcook). Set aside.

Melt 3 tablespoons of butter, and stir in 1 tablespoon of flour to make a roux. Pour in the juice from the cooked lobster. Pour in the cream, a few dribs at a time, stirring till smooth and thickened. Take off the heat.

This part is tricky. If you're using the egg yolks to thicken the sauce, put the cream sauce in the top of a double boiler. Let it cool a bit but not so much it starts to set up. Beat the eggs in a separate bowl, and add a tiny bit of the cream sauce, being careful not to let the eggs curdle. Keep adding the cream sauce until you've used it all, and then put the whole mixture back in the top of the double boiler and heat over hot water for approximately 3 minutes. Do not let the water or sauce boil. Turn off the heat. Fold in the lobster. Season to taste. Turn into a greased deep-dish pie pan, and cover with topping. Bake for 10 to 15 minutes in a low oven (300 to 325 degrees, depending on how hot your oven cooks).

If you don't want to use the egg yolks, you can thicken the cream sauce with 3 or 4 slices of white bread with the crusts cut off. Tear into pieces and fold into the cream sauce together with the lobster. Season to taste. Turn into greased pie dish and bake 30 minutes at 350 degrees.

*Season to taste with salt, pepper, and paprika. Sheriff Mort Metzger's wife likes to add $\frac{1}{4}$ teaspoon of dry mustard. I like to add 1 tablespoon of sautéed shallots or Vidalia onion.

**Top with a mixture of crumbled crackers, a dry grated cheese like Parmesan (a tablespoon or two) and softened butter (a heaping $\frac{1}{4}$ cup of dry ingredients to 2 tablespoons of butter). Oyster crackers are perfect. Ritz crackers make it very rich. Seth likes it when I add a few crushed potato chips. Sprinkle in a little extra paprika for color. You may want to skip the topping if you use bread to thicken the pie.

For lobster stew, add sautéed celery, mushrooms and/or cooked carrots, and cut back on the thickening and omit topping. Great over rice.

Well-known mystery writer Jessica Fletcher, star of the "Murder, She Wrote" television series, has twenty published novels (co-authored with Donald Bain). Look for *Majoring in Murder, You Bet Your Life, Provence—To Die For*, and other titles in the "Murder, She Wrote" series.

Annapolis Fish Stew

MARCIA TALLEY

When Annapolitan and sleuth, Hannah Ives (*Sing It To Her Bones, Unbreathed Memories, Occasion of Revenge*) is in the mood for crab cakes, she goes to McGarveys; when she hankers after traditional Irish stew, it's Galway Bay. But, when the wind blows cold off the Chesapeake Bay and fish stew is on the menu, Hannah takes a brisk walk down Prince George Street to City Dock, where sea-going vessels have docked for centuries and where, since 1788, the Market House has been providing "all accommodations necessary for the reception and sale of provisions." After warming her hands on a cappuccino at City Dock Café, Hannah heads for the Annapolis Fish Market to select fresh fish for her popular stew.

8 cups water
3 medium potatoes, peeled, cut into ¼-inch cubes
3 medium turnips, cut into ¼-inch cubes
4 large carrots, cut into ¼-inch cubes
2 celery stalks, thinly sliced (including tops)
3 medium or 2 large leeks, thinly sliced (both white and green parts, thoroughly
    rinsed in cold water)
2 pounds any firm-fleshed ocean fish such as grouper, cod, halibut, porgy, or
    whiting, cut into 2-inch chunks
4 generous sprigs fresh cilantro (coriander), chopped
1 teaspoon black pepper
½ teaspoon salt or to taste

Put the water and vegetables in a large pot, bring to a boil, and simmer for 10 minutes. Add the fish and seasonings, and simmer for 30 minutes more. Serve topped with garlic bread crumbs, if desired. Delicious with white rice.

Makes 6 to 8 servings.

Author Marcia Talley says if she doubles the recipe, it'd be enough to serve all twelve co-conspirators in her wild and wacky serial novels, *Naked Came the Phoenix* and *Naked Came the Gryphon*. Learn more about her at www.marciatalley.com.

Florence's Sautéed Brook Trout With Lime

EVAN MARSHALL

*I*n my Jane Stuart and Winky mysteries, which are set in New Jersey, Jane has a wonderful nanny named Florence who comes from Trinidad. Florence is always cooking up dishes from home, often substituting New Jersey ingredients for Trinidad ones. New Jersey meets the Caribbean in this recipe featuring brook trout, New Jersey's state fish. This dish is a favorite at my house.

 1 pound brook trout fillets, about ½ inch thick
 1 cup all-purpose flour
 Salt and pepper
 2 small cloves garlic, minced
 ½ cup dry white wine
 1 tablespoon fresh lime juice
 1 teaspoon butter
 1 tablespoon olive oil
 3 scallions, chopped
 Lime wedges for garnish

Rinse the fish and pat dry. Put the flour on a plate, and season with salt and pepper. Dredge the fish fillets in the flour, patting to remove excess. Combine the garlic, wine, lime juice, and butter in a small bowl. Heat the olive oil in a large skillet over medium-high heat. Add the fillets without overlapping (you may need to cook in more than one batch). Cook until golden on bottom, about 3 minutes. Turn and cook until opaque through the center, 1 to 2 minutes more. Transfer to a platter, and cover with foil to keep warm. Add wine mixture to the pan and bring to a boil, scraping up the cooked bits, until reduced by half, about 2 to 3 minutes. Stir in the scallions and heat about 30 seconds. Pour the sauce over the fish, garnish with lime wedges, and serve with new potatoes, French green beans, rolls and butter, and a chilled white Burgundy like Fumé Blanc.

Evan Marshall is the author of the Jane Stuart and Winky mysteries—most recently *Stabbing Stephanie*, *Icing Ivy*, and *Toasting Tina*. He can be reached through his website, www.The Novelist.com.

Josie's Salmon Patties

SHARON SHORT

*I*n *Death of a Domestic Diva*, Josie Toadfern—stain expert and laundromat owner with a penchant for nosiness—decides to get a little publicity for her hometown of Paradise, Ohio by inviting herself on the popular Tyra Grimes Home Show. Tyra, a self-made expert in all things domestic, turns the tables by showing up in Paradise unannounced. Soon, she has Paradisites one and all eating out of her hand—for example, feeding them salmon canapés while giving them tips on how to make seasonal mulch. Sure, Josie knows Paradise is really a salmon patty kind of town…but when murder and mayhem ensue, can she convince her fellow Paradisites to help her set things right?

> 1 14 ¾ ounce can salmon, drained (Josie recommends fancy pink salmon)
> 4 slices white bread, torn into crumbs
> 2 eggs
> 2 teaspoon Worcestershire sauce
> 1 teaspoon dry mustard
> ½ teaspoon salt
> 2 tablespoon vegetable oil

Thoroughly mix all but the oil until the ingredients are well blended. Shape into 8 patties. Fry in oil over medium heat until golden brown on both sides, 4 to 5 minutes.

Serve with homemade tartar sauce—1 tablespoon pickle relish mixed with 3 tablespoons mayonnaise.

Josie's favorite side dish with salmon patties: white hominy, heated through.

Sharon Short is the author of a new humorous mystery series featuring Josie Toadfern, stain expert and laundromat owner in Paradise, Ohio. The first novel in the series is *Death of a Domestic Diva*.

Tequila Shrimp

L.C. HAYDEN

Both my character Harry Bronson and his wife, Carol, had lived through an especially hard week. They agreed that tonight, they'd go out to eat. Harry wanted seafood. Carol said, "No, Mexican." They argued and thought maybe Italian as a way of compromising. They stormed out of the house, neither happy with the compromise. That day, Harry got home early and prepared Tequila Shrimp and, to add a touch of Italy, he served it on a bed of fresh pasta. Carol was delighted.

> 1 ½ pounds jumbo shrimp
> ½ cup butter (1 stick)
> 6 cloves garlic, chopped
> 3 ounces gold tequila
> Pinch of kosher salt
> Juice of 3 limes
> 1 tablespoon fresh cilantro
> 1 tablespoon crushed red pepper (optional)

Wash, shell, and de-vein shrimp, set aside.

In a large skillet, sauté the butter and garlic over medium-low heat. Add the tequila and salt. Mix until well blended. Bring the heat up to medium. Add the shrimp. Cook for 5 to 7 minutes, stirring and tossing until shrimp is bright pinkish orange and firm. Add the lime juice and cilantro, and crushed pepper if desired; toss once more before serving.

Serve as an appetizer with some fancy toothpicks, or over a bed of fresh pasta or rice. It is delicious, smooth and buttery.

L.C. Hayden's Harry Bronson mysteries include *What Others Know*, *Where Secrets Lie*, and *Who's Susan?* Visit http://lchayden.freeservers.com.

Chesapeake Bay Crab Cakes
KIT EHRMAN

Since my protagonist, Steve Cline, is a Maryland native, there's one delicacy he's sure to indulge in every summer: Chesapeake Bay Crab Cakes. You're not a Marylander if you don't enjoy crab cakes and a cold brew once in a while. Now, this is not to say that he would make them himself. His idea of cooking consists of heating a can of Dinty Moore Stew on the stove. He's only twenty-one, after all. But I have no doubt his girlfriend, the alluring Rachel, would make them for him.

>   1 pound backfin crabmeat
>   3 tablespoons mayonnaise
>   1 teaspoon ground mustard
>   1 rib celery, finely chopped
>   1 green onion, finely chopped
>   ½ teaspoon Old Bay Seasoning (or ½ teaspoon paprika)
>   Parsley
>   1 egg, beaten
>   Italian bread crumbs
>   2 tablespoons vegetable oil
>   6 onion Kaiser rolls
>   Tartar sauce

Mix together the mayonnaise, ground mustard, celery, green onion, Old Bay Seasoning, egg, and parsley. Set aside.

Check the crabmeat and remove any cartilage pieces. Fold the crabmeat into the ingredients above.

Gently shape into 6 ¾-inch thick patties, and coat with bread crumbs. Refrigerate for 30 minutes.

Spray a skillet with nonstick cooking spray, and add the vegetable oil. Cook the crab cakes in skillet over medium-high heat for 3 to 4 minutes each side, or until lightly browned.

Serve on onion Kaiser rolls with tartar sauce. Makes 6 servings

Kit Ehrman is the author of *At Risk,* a Steve Cline mystery set in Maryland horse country, where managing a show barn can be murder. Her website can be found at www.kitehrman.com.

Shrimp Salad Savannah
VONDA SKINNER SKELTON

*T*welve-year-old Bitsy has had a vacation to remember at Tybee Island, Georgia. She not only dug up a skeleton and survived a kidnapping, but she also solved the robbery of Williams Seafood Restaurant in Savannah. To reward her bravery, Tommy and Wanda Williams treat the young heroine and her family to a delicious meal, starting with their famous shrimp salad. It is the beginning of a most memorable evening.

> 1 pound cooked, peeled, and de-veined shrimp (medium are best)
> 1 cup sweet pickle relish, squeezed/drained very well
> 2 hard boiled eggs, chopped
> 1 cup mayonnaise
> Salt and pepper to taste
> Lettuce

Chop the shrimp into small pieces. Add the other ingredients. Mix well. Chill before serving. Serve on a bed of lettuce with crackers on side.

Serves 4.

Vonda Skinner Skelton is the author of the children's mystery, *Bitsy and The Mystery at Tybee Island.*

Blini

(Russian Pancakes)

ELLEN CROSBY

*I*n my first novel *Moscow Nights*, Claire Brennan, my main character, dines on blini filled with caviar and sour cream at a Moscow restaurant with a man with whom she once had an affair. I suppose blini—probably the most popular and classic of Russian foods—have always been associated with romance and special occasions for me, as my Russian/French husband fixed this dish for me on one of our first dates. Ever since it has been a celebratory meal in our home.

> 2 ½ cups lukewarm milk
> 1 package active dry yeast
> 1 cup white flour
> 1 cup buckwheat flour
> 3 tablespoons sugar
> ½ teaspoon salt
> 6 tablespoons unsalted butter, melted and cooled
> 3 eggs, lightly beaten
> Melted butter for frying

In a small bowl, combine the warm milk and yeast. Whisk to dissolve. In a large bowl combine the white flour, buckwheat flour, sugar, and salt. Add the milk and yeast mixture, melted butter, and eggs to the flour mixture. Beat until smooth.

Cover the bowl with a towel, and put it in a warm place to let rise or 1 to 1 ½ hours, or until doubled in bulk.

Heat oven to 200 degrees to keep blini warm while others are being fried.

Preheat a frying pan over medium heat, and brush *very lightly* with melted butter. We use a 6-inch pan and make one blini at a time.

Pour about 3 tablespoons of batter evenly into the pan, and fry until golden brown, about 1 minute; turn and cook for another 30 seconds. Repeat with the rest of the batter, brushing the pan with butter as needed. Keep blini warm in the oven on a heat-proof plate until all are cooked.

Fill with:
- 1 pound caviar (an expense nearly equivalent to buying 1 pound of diamonds; you might splurge, however, on an ounce or two since caviar goes so well with blini)
  or
- ½ to 1 pound assorted salted or smoked fish such as salmon, sturgeon, herring, etc.
  or
- Chopped mushrooms, lightly sautéed with butter and herbs

Serve with:

¾ cup hot melted unsalted butter and/or 2 cups sour cream

Serve as you would a crepe or jelly roll: spread sour cream or pour butter on the blini, place fish, mushrooms, or caviar in the center and roll up.

Yield: Approximately 12 to 18 6-inch blini, which can serve 4 to 6 as an entrée or 8 to 10 as an appetizer.

Drink with:

Shots of ice-cold vodka such as Stolichnaya or Grey Goose (flavored or plain), which has been well-chilled in the freezer.

Ellen Crosby made her mystery-writing debut with *Moscow Nights*, featuring Claire Brennan.

MURDER MOST FOWL

Hitchcock Sewell's "Coq Au Dad"

TIM COCKEY

*H*itchcock Sewell's swill of choice is usually Maker's Mark, but there are times when a chef has to make do with the ingredients on hand. The first time I attempted to make the original version of this recipe I discovered that I didn't have the red wine on hand that was called for. I did, however, have a bottle of Old Grand Dad Kentucky Bourbon at the ready. Readers of my series might know Hitch as a boiled hot dogs-for-dinner and waffles-for-breakfast kind of guy…but now and again he shows a fancier hand. This one is right up his dark alley.

> 3 tablespoons flour
> 1 teaspoon salt
> ½ teaspoon paprika
> ⅛ teaspoon nutmeg
> 4 slices bacon
> ¼ cup butter
> 1 3-pound chicken, killed and cut up
> 1 cup sliced mushrooms
> 1, 2, 3, however many you want, cloves garlic, minced
> ¼ teaspoon thyme
> ¼ teaspoon marjoram
> 1 small bay leaf (why? who knows?)
> ¼ cup brandy
> A couple of handfuls of small white onions
> 1 cup Old Grand Dad Kentucky Bourbon
> Chopped parsley

This is one of those dishes that taste better the next day. So the first thing you do is to order a pizza and crack open a bottle of beer so as to make certain that you don't have any appetite issues getting in the way. Django Reinhardt is probably the kind of music you'll want to put on while you make this dish. You want something that is loose and free, so that you will feel liberal and what-the-hell-ish when it comes to the stirring and spicing.

Mix the flour, salt, paprika, and nutmeg in a Peruvian mixing bowl. If you don't have a Peruvian mixing bowl, finish off your beer and start on a new one. Then don't worry about it. Cook the bacon. Remove it when crisp. Add the butter and melt it with the bacon grease, and then brown the chicken in this glorious cholesterol-enhancer. Throw in the mushrooms, the garlic, and the herbs. Cook over moderate heat until you hear the mushrooms saying "ouch! ouch! ouch!" Go into the bedroom and put on an ascot (if you are a man), killer pumps and very red lipstick (if you are a woman); or mix and match (this is not really any of my business), then return to the kitchen, crack open the bottle of brandy, pour a short short glass of it, take a seat, wave the glass under your nose, then get back to the oven, warm the brandy in a small pan and pour it over the chicken. Ignite at once (keep the ascot clear) and when the flame dies down, add the onions and mix gently. Uncork the Old Grand Dad Kentucky

Bourbon (with your teeth if you're so inclined), pour a healthy cup of it over the chicken, cover it and cook it over low flame for about an hour.

Change out of your silly clothes and go out for a nice evening. The next day, invite people over, heat the concoction back up, then just before serving sprinkle with minced parsley and the crispy bacon bits. Serve on a table, with chairs nearby.

Tim Cockey's so-called "hearse series," featuring dashing and dizzy-headed Baltimore undertaker Hitchcock Sewell, includes *The Hearse You Came In On*, *Hearse of a Different Color* and *Murder in the Hearse Degree*. Visit him at http://www.timcockey.com.

Chicken-Almond Puffs

SHARAN NEWMAN

*T*his recipe is my own invention. I'd give you something from the twelfth century but I've never seen a cookbook from that period. However, there's nothing in this that a well-to-do medieval cook couldn't have found and they were very fond of chopped meat in pastry. The spice and nut mixture is also something they might do, to help keep the meat unidentifiable. My main character, Catherine, really isn't much of a cook, so she would either have her cook make these or, more likely, buy them from a bake shop or pastry stand in Paris. Some things never change.

So, for the puffs, preheat oven to 425 degrees.

1 cup chicken broth	1 cup flour
6 tablespoons butter*	4 eggs
1 teaspoon salt	

Heat the broth and butter with the salt until it comes to a rolling boil. Add the flour all at once and stir vigorously. It will pull away from the edge of the pan and look a bit like thick mashed potatoes. Now add the eggs one at a time. No fudging and throwing them in all at once. After you add each egg, stir until it is all blended in before you add the next. It only takes a minute or so but you need to be firm. Don't let the egg slide around but make it incorporate into the dough.

OK, now put the dough by teaspoonful on a cookie sheet. You don't need to grease it. The puffs should be about the size of a walnut (in the shell). Bake for 20 minutes or so. They should puff nicely and be brown on the top. Sometimes I turn off the oven and let them sit another 5 minutes just to be sure.

While the puffs are baking, make the filling.

1 cup chopped, peeled almonds	2 teaspoons flour
2 tablespoons butter*	1 cup chopped cooked chicken
1 teaspoon mace (that's a spice, not a weapon)	¼ cup cream

* You can use margarine but it won't taste as good. The same goes for the cream.

Melt the butter in a skillet and brown the almonds, stirring constantly. Add the mace and flour, and cook a bit more, to let them brown. Add the chicken and mix well. It should be fairly thick. Finally stir in the cream.

Slice the puffs three-quarters of the way through, and fill with the chicken mixture.

This may seem like a lot of work, but it's less than an hour. Also, you can make the puffs and filling a day or more ahead and just put them together at the last minute. The puffs also freeze well and are good for impressive instant hors d'oeuvres. You can fill them with all kinds of stuff.

Sharan Newman writes the Catherine LeVendeur mysteries. The last three, in reverse order are: *The Outcast Dove, Heresy,* and *To Wear the White Cloak.*

Goody Anne's Chicken And Vegetable Pie

ALYS CLARE

*I*n my Hawkenlye novels, the hostess of Josse d'Acquin's favorite tavern enjoys a reputation for "good, honest nourishment, cooked fresh every day." It is no fault of Goody Anne's that in *The Tavern in the Morning,* the third in the series, a man dies after enjoying a meal at the inn; his dish of chicken pie was poisoned with wolf's bane.

Goody Anne would have made her pies in the medieval way, with a raised crust. The pastry, made from flour and water, served as a container for the contents and was not normally eaten. The filling would have been whatever the lad had found in the market: chicken, pork, game, perhaps hare but rarely rabbit since these were brought into England by the Normans and were still pretty much a delicacy. The medieval taste seems to have been for a touch of sweetness mixed in with savory dishes.

Here, without the wolf's bane, is a modern-day version of Josse's favorite pie.

Pastry

> 1 ⅔ cup all-purpose flour
> ½ cup less 1 tablespoon of fat (butter or margarine and lard), softened
> Cold water

Mix the flour and butter together thoroughly. Add water if it appears too thick to roll into a ball.

Roll out the pastry dough and use roughly half to line a deep 8-inch round pie dish (the remainder will form the pie's lid).

Filling

> 1 medium-size chicken
> Sage, thyme, salt, pepper to season
> 2 to 3 cloves of garlic
> 2 medium onions
> 2 large carrots
> Small bulb of fennel
> A little oil (for frying)
> 1 large cooking apple
> Lemon juice
> 1 pound good sausage meat
> 1 to 2 tablespoons single cream
> Glaze of beaten egg

Preheat the oven to 400 degrees.

Skin the chicken, and cut the meat into smallish cubes. Season well with salt, pepper, and the herbs.

Peel and crush the garlic with a little salt. Peel and chop the onions and carrots. Cut up the fennel. Heat a little oil in a pan and briefly brown the garlic and chopped vegetables. Remove from heat and allow to cool. Peel, core, and chop the apple, turn it in the lemon juice (Goody Anne might have added honey for sweetness), and add to the browned vegetables. Stir the cream into the sausage meat and combine with the vegetables, stirring till all is well mixed. Put half of the mixture into the pastry-lined pie dish. Put the cubed chicken on top, then the remainder of the sausage meat and vegetable mix. Cover with the pastry lid, sealing the edges well. Brush with beaten egg.

Bake the pie on a baking sheet at 400 degrees for 30 minutes, then turn the oven down to 350 degrees, and back for a further 90 minutes.

Serves 6 to 8.

Alys Clare's Hawkenlye Mysteries include *The Faithful Dead* and *A Dark Night Hidden*.

Eintopfgericht Von Ratteriesse

RICHARD A. LUPOFF

When I was in the US Army in 1956 I was assigned to the faculty of The Adjutant General's School near Indianapolis, Indiana. I lived in Bachelor Officers' Quarters (BOQ) along with other staff and faculty members and students assigned to the school. Many of our students came from friendly nations, and in due course an informal gourmet society was formed, in which officers from China, Ecuador, Korea, Japan, Turkey, the Phillipines, and Wisconsin took turns in preparing dishes of their native lands.

Two of my friends were Soemardi Suradareja and Joesoef Natasukma, both majors in the army of the Republic of Indonesia, both from the city of Jakarta. Around the BOQ they preferred to be known as Joe and Sam. Joe was handsome and outgoing. He loved American culture and accumulated a choice collection of jazz records to take home at the end of his assignment in the United States. Sam was slim and wiry, a quiet man and I suspect a deep thinker.

As happens so often, the person who learns the most in school is the teacher. From Joe and Sam I learned that Jakartans consider themselves the most sophisticated and progressive of Indonesians. They hold themselves above all other Javanese, and all Javanese hold themselves above all other Indonesians, regarding residents of the "out islands" as the Southwestern Pacific equivalent of hillbillies. Sumatra is one of the lesser islands of Indonesia, but it is the source of the world's finest giant rats.

From Joe and Sam I also learned to prepare *Eintopfgericht von Ratteriesse,* or Giant Rat of Sumatra Stew. It made a remarkably delicious meal. On one occasion the three of us were working as a team in the BOQ kitchen when I asked, "Isn't Indonesia a Muslim country?"

Sam replied, "Yes."

"Doesn't Islam forbid the consumption of alcoholic beverages?"

Joe answered, "Yes."

"But there's bourbon in the stew."

Sam and Joe smiled and in unison said, "When in Rome…"

But in fact once the bourbon has boiled even briefly the alcoholic content of the stew is small or nil, while the bouquet is exquisite and the meal is delicious.

Nota bene: If giant Sumatran rat is unavailable, it is not recommended that you substitute common or domestic *rattus rattus.* Instead, try the recipe with chicken.

Use all ingredients and follow directions as below:

> 1 giant Sumatran rat (skinned)
> 3 large yellow onions
> 4 to 6 medium-size carrots
> 4 cloves garlic
> ½ cup olive oil
> 1 cup sugar, mixed with 2 tablespoons salt
> 1 small bottle soy sauce
> 1 to 2 cups fine Bourbon whiskey

Slice the rat into pieces convenient for consuming as "finger food."

Fill a family-size stew pot with sufficient water to cover the ingredients.

Slice the onions. Clean the carrots but do not slice. Slice the garlic into slivers.

Using a sharp kitchen knife, pierce the rat meat, and insert 1 sliver of garlic into each opening. Rub the rat with olive oil, then rub in the mixture of sugar and salt until absorbed by meat.

Bring the water in the pot to boil, adding the soy sauce and any surplus olive oil. Add the vegetables, and permit to stew for 20 to 30 minutes.

Add the rat. When the rat meat turns grayish-white (this should take only about 5 minutes), add the Bourbon. Let boil for 1 to 2 minutes longer.

Serve over a bed of boiled brown rice.

Richard A. Lupoff is the author of many books including the Hobart Lindsey/Marvia Plum mysteries—*The Silver Chariot Killer, The Radio Red Killer, One Murder at a Time: The Case Book of Lindsey and Plum*—and such nonfiction works as *The Great American Paperback*.

Yakibuck

DAVID FULMER

A year ago, I was invited, along with my friend Robert Skinner, to do a signing at Jazz Fest in New Orleans. It turned out that Emeril was on ahead of us, so for at least a half-hour after we took over the signing table, people kept stepping up to stare at me, point accusing fingers and say, "Hey, you're not Emeril!"

"Well, no, I'm not, thank you very much. I'm also not chopped liver; and as a single parent, it so happens I've got some game in the kitchen."

When I started writing *Chasing the Devil's Tail*, the critical issues were: cheap, easy and tasty, in that order. An accident evolved into my go-to dish, a twice-a-week standby through those first-draft months. Since then, I've made it for others and it's garnered great reviews every time. Even my six-year-old loves it.

Use only dark meat chicken (or turkey or duck). White meat gets too dry. So we're talking leg quarters or thighs. It works better with the bones in, so you don't have to buy boneless cuts. We're talking the down-and-dirty end of the meat department here. It also doesn't work with the skin on, which has an added health benefit. So start by removing the skin and as much fat as you can see. Use the funkiest piece of bakeware you can lay your hands on. I use an old nonstick pie pan that is encrusted with god-knows-what by this point. It won't come off. But it sure seems to add something to the recipe and now I'm superstitious about it. Bake the chicken at 300 degrees for 15 to 20 minutes, until all the pink is gone. Then take it out of the oven and using a sharp knife (heh heh heh), make 2 or 3 parallel slits, 2 or 3 inches in length, as deep as you can go without coming out the underside. Call them slashes if it puts you in the spirit.

Pour Lite Teriyaki Sauce all over the chicken, especially down in those slits. Use the Lite—the regular is too much. Stick it back in the oven. Pop in every 15 minutes or so to do a quick baste with one of those little brushes. You can add a little water or some more sauce to keep it liquid. Bake it until it gets a dark copper color. This will take about 40 minutes, though it's pretty hard to overcook it. Sometimes, when I was in a rush, I turned the oven up to 450 to hurry it along and it still came out fine. You can even put it in the broiler, though I wouldn't advise leaving it there unless you have an interest in arson. You can also turn the heat way down and, as long as you keep it moist, it will wait, as patiently as a private eye's secretary, until you're good and ready. Really, it's hard to destroy this one. When it's close, you can throw some pineapple chunks in there, too.

You can serve it with anything. We usually opt for rice and a vegetable. There will be sauce in the pan to pour over the rice. It reheats well and I've eaten it cold, too. How something so simple to make can taste so good is a mystery to me. I do know that the elements are important, as they are in any crime. Change one and it changes the entire outcome.

Chasing the Devil's Tail, David Fulmer's first published novel, won a Shamus Award and was nominated for a *Los Angeles Times* Book Prize and a Barry Award.

Ground Chicken Mystery

TIM MYERS

I'd like to share one of my own personal favorite recipes. Being a brand new Stay-at-Home Dad, I had several shocks to my system the first day I started my 'new job' in 1991, not the least of which was being responsible for the family dinner menu! I'd dabbled some with cooking before, but it became serious business with our newly reduced income. Hey, I'm not complaining, because as a direct result of raising my daughter at home, I became a mystery writer, and I've gone on to sell over 70 short stories as well as 2 mystery series! Over time, I grew confident enough to start trying out my own recipes. This is one we like best.

> 1 pound ground chicken
> 1 small onion, diced
> 1 tablespoon olive oil
> 1 can green beans
> 2 baking potatoes
> 8 ounces shredded cheese (I like mozzarella and cheddar blends myself)

Brown the ground chicken and diced onion in olive oil, then drain.

Mash the potatoes just like you normally would. (I like to make mine from scratch.) Heat the green beans.

When everything's ready, place the chicken/onion combo in the bottom of a large ovenproof casserole dish. Next add a layer of green beans (I've used peas and limas in a pinch, but my family likes green beans the best). Next, layer the mashed potatoes across the top, then top it all off with the shredded cheese. Bake at 375 degrees for 15 minutes, or until the cheese melts and browns slightly to your satisfaction.

This is a foolproof recipe that is one of my family's favorites. Total baking and preparation time is 40 minutes.

Serves 4.

Tim Myers is the author of the Lighthouse Inn Mystery series featuring Agatha Award Nominee *Innkeeping with Murder, Reservations for Murder* and *Murder Checks Inn*, as well as the new Candleshop Mystery series featuring *At Wick's End.*

Liam's Chicken Tostada

NAOMI RAND

Being a single mom, and the mother of two, my main protagonist, Emma Price has a lot on her plate. When all else fails, and she can't get her older son's good will, she stoops to bribery. Liam's favorite dish is faux Mexican, and Emma knows when to cook it, and how far it goes towards soothing the savage teenage beast.

> 1 whole frying or roasting chicken, average size, preferably Bell and Evans or free range (for taste)
> 2 cloves of garlic, chopped
> Kosher salt
> Oregano
> 2 ripe tomatoes
> Fresh coriander (cilantro)
> 2 Bermuda onions, diced
> 1 jalapeño pepper
> 2 ripe avocados (dark and soft to the touch)
> Balsamic vinegar
> Olive oil
> Black beans, canned and cooked
> 2 ears corn or a can of pre-cooked corn
> Garlic flakes
> Sour cream
> 1 lemon
> Pepper
> Cheddar cheese
> A package of twelve uncooked corn tortillas
> Cooking oil or lard
> Salonika peppers in brine vinegar
> Pitted olives (any type you like)
> Hot sauce, green or red

Sprinkle the chicken with chopped garlic, kosher salt, and oregano. Put in a roasting pan and set the oven at 375 degrees. Roast the chicken until cooked through, about an hour and a quarter. If you can pull the leg back and the meat separates from the bone without blood, then it's done.

Meanwhile, make the salsa. Chop the tomatoes in cubes, add $\frac{1}{4}$ teaspoon of diced garlic, diced cilantro, and diced red onions, a smidgen of diced jalapeño pepper, and cube half of a ripe avocado. Put together in a bowl. Add a dash of balsamic vinegar, and 2 dashes of olive oil. Mix and taste. Add salt to taste. Set aside or refrigerate.

To prepare the beans: Put a tablespoon of olive oil in a pan and heat, add $\frac{1}{2}$ to 1 teaspoon of diced garlic, $\frac{1}{8}$ cup of diced onions, and the beans. Cook until heated through, set aside, and reheat just before serving.

Cut the kernels off the ears of corn with a sharp knife, in rows. Heat a tablespoon of olive oil, ¼ teaspoon of garlic flakes, a bit of diced cilantro, and as it cooks add the corn. Add water as you stir, if it sticks to the bottom. If using canned corn, no water necessary. Cook until it heats, or if fresh, until the corn is cooked through, about 4 minutes, then set aside, and heat again before serving.

For the guacamole: Use 1 to 1 ½ avocados, depending on how much guacamole you like to slather on your tostada. Mash the avocado, add ¼ teaspoon of chopped garlic, a bit of chopped onion to taste, a smidgen of diced jalepeño to taste, and a teaspoon of diced coriander. Mash with sour cream until creamy enough, then add the juice of ½ lemon, to taste. A dash of salt, a grind of pepper. Refrigerate.

Grate the cheese until it fills a small bowl and refrigerate.

Fry the tortillas: Make sure the oil is hot, then drop the tortillas in till they are crisp on one side, turn and fry till crisp on the other side, drain on a plate with a paper towel. Cook them flat.

Put the Salonika peppers, the olives, and everything else out on the table. Cut the chicken off the bone. Layer the tostada, chicken first, in strips of meat, and then whatever else appeals to you. Now take a bite....

I guarantee, that if you serve this, your errant teen will be home for dinner. The only trouble is, he might bring his friends.

Will feed 4 adults, or 1 ravenous teen.

Liam, Emma, and her second child, Katherine Rose, appear in *The One That Got Away* and *Stealing for a Living*. Visit www.naomirand.com.

Aaron Tucker's Oven Fried Chicken

JEFFREY COHEN

People who know me read my first novel and say, "Oh, that's you," as if they expected the main character to be much more like Marcel Proust. But he's not me; he's like me. His circumstances are the same: he's a freelance writer who works out of his home and has a son and a daughter. His wife is an attorney (although in a much different branch of law than my wife practices). He lives in New Jersey.

Authors tend to defend themselves like Ophelia, protesting too much (or was that Lady Macbeth? Or Sheena, Queen of the Jungle?), but this is the truth: Aaron is a version of me, the me I wish I could be, who is braver, smarter, funnier and generally better looking than I am. He also solves the occasional murder mystery, which I have thankfully never been called upon to do. That's why we call it fiction, friends.

Now, there is one more similarity. One of the things Aaron says in the book is "I know about cooking what Dr. Seuss knew about the Great American Novel—how to do it for kids." I can make a grand total of four dishes: baked macaroni and cheese, meat loaf, pasta (which really is the same as macaroni and cheese with a few steps removed), and the following chicken dish, which I substitute for the high-fat, deep fried version my kids would actually prefer. I work at home, so I end up doing a good deal of the cooking for the children. My wife cooks for herself and me, since she refuses to eat anything I know how to cook, and I don't blame her.

For kids though, this is a lower-fat version of something they might already like.

1 ½ cups bread crumbs or matzo meal	Onion salt (nobody said it would be
Salt	low sodium!)
Pepper	¼ cup Egg Beaters (or similar product)
Chopped onion	1 pound boneless, skinless chicken breast
Garlic	

Preheat oven to 400 degrees.

In one bowl, combine the bread crumbs (or matzo meal), salt, pepper, chopped onion, garlic, onion salt, all to taste. Mix well. Put in some more salt if your kids are used to the Colonel (it is my opinion that 8 out of his 11 herbs and spices are salt).

In a second bowl, pour the egg product. Cut the chicken into strips about 2 inches wide. Roll each strip in the egg product, then dredge in bread crumbs (or matzo meal) mixture. Don't be shy about coating; it's the part the kids actually want to eat.

Place the strips on a cookie sheet that has been pre-treated with cooking spray (the heck with the ozone layer!). You can put them on aluminum foil, too, if you're into that sort of thing.

Bake at 400 degrees for 25 minutes, or until cooked through and browned, turning once. Serve with oven baked French fries or rice, or something. I'm not planning your whole meal for you.

Go read another mystery!

Jeffrey Cohen has written the Aaron Tucker mysteries *A Farewell to Legs* and *For Whom the Minivan Rolls*.

Publish...Or Perish?

After Poisoned Pen Press came onboard as the publisher of this esteemed volume, we met Barbara Peters at Left Coast Crime in Pasadena.

"Has Robert given you his recipe for deep-fried turkey?" she asked almost before she had finished shaking hands.

Robert, of course, is Robert Rosenwald, intrepid independent publisher and, by all accounts, great cook. (Oh, and Barbara's husband, too.)

No, we admitted, he hadn't. Did she think we could pry it out of him?

"Ask him," Barbara said, though the gleam in her eye told us it wasn't going to take a Sicilian hit man to strong arm the recipe out of him.

Robert did protest that he wasn't a mystery author, but hey, he's many a mystery author's best ally. Ours, too.

Deep Fried Turkey
ROBERT ROSENWALD

15 pound turkey
25 Bay leaves
1 tablespoon dried thyme
1 tablespoon dried oregano
2 teaspoons black peppercorns
3 tablespoons hot Creole seasoning
2 teaspoons garlic powder
2 teaspoons cayenne pepper
Peanut oil

Wash the turkey, pat dry. Finely grind the bay leaves in a spice grinder; transfer to a small bowl. Finely grind the thyme, oregano, and peppercorns; add to the bay leaves. Mix in the Creole seasoning, garlic powder, and cayenne. Rub ⅓ of the spice mix in the inside of turkey, ⅓ under the skin of the breasts, and ⅓ on the outside. Place the turkey in a plastic bag and marinate overnight, or up to 72 hours in the refrigerator.

Bring the turkey to room temperature. Use a wooden skewer to thread the neck flap to the bottom of the turkey. Truss the legs and pope's nose with wire.

Heat 5 gallons of peanut oil or other deep-frying shortening oil to 360 degrees. Deep fry *outdoors* over a propane burner in a 40 quart stock pot or a turkey fryer (obtainable online and from various outdoor sporting suppliers) for 3 minutes per pound. *Do not overcook.* Let stand for 20 minutes before carving.

Serves 10.

MEATING OUT JUSTICE

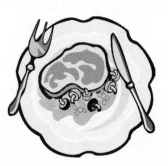

Spicy Lamb Casserole
ROBERT BARNARD

I cannot remember any dish in my books that I would be able to give a foolproof recipe for. Most of my characters eat in restaurants, and fairly straightforward dishes. When I have had scenes of eating at home the meals are often intended to be comic, and would probably be disgusting if tried.

Some of my best memories are eating in restaurants. Maybe the most recent one is ending a meal in a Parma *ristorante* (once Parma was full of wonderful eating places, but these have been decimated) with a request for Gorgonzola. I was already full, and this was a piece of piggery. I staggered when cheese the size of several bricks arrived, and it turned out to be the most wonderful creamy Gorgonzola I had ever tasted—I should have picked at it and sent it away regretfully, but I charged into it and emerged (probably) an hour later, blissfully happy. But that is Italy. No other country (no, not even the unmentionable country to their north) can eat so happily and well.

Here is a recipe I am fond of, because I like chucking lots of things into a pot, turning the oven on, then going away and doing something else, like listening to music (Italian preferably) or plotting sudden death.

> 2 meaty lamb shanks
> 1 cup chopped onions, already fried in butter
> A small can of whole or chopped tomatoes
> 2 cloves garlic, chopped fine or minced
> Salt and pepper to taste
> 2 tablespoons paprika
> Some oregano or basil
> ½ cup port or Marsala
> ½ cup stock

Place the lamb shanks in a casserole and add all of the other ingredients. Heat the oven to 350 degrees and shove the casserole in, covered, for about an hour and a half, basting when you remember. Turn down the oven to 250 degrees, remove the cover, and cook until you are ready to eat, about three-quarters of an hour to an hour, if it is not to go dry.

Serves 2.

Just a few of the books by the prolific Robert Barnard are *A Scandal in Belgravia, A Murder in Mayfair, School for Murder,* and *The Mistress of Alderley.*

Lamb to the Slaughter

*At that point, Mary Maloney simply walked up behind him and
without any pause she swung the big frozen leg of lamb high in the air
and brought it down as hard as she could on the back of his head....*

*She carried the meat into the kitchen, placed it in a pan,
turned the oven on high, and shoved it inside.*

The apotheosis of the culinary crime story may be "Lamb to the Slaughter," Roald Dahl's ghoulish tale in which a mousy, pregnant housewife fells her philandering policeman husband with a frozen leg of lamb. She then cooks up the evidence and serves it to her husband's friends—the police who come to investigate the killing. Could there be any better way to dispose of a murder weapon than to eat it?

Roast Leg of Lamb

Preheat oven to 450 degrees with rack placed in lower third of oven.

5-7 pound leg of lamb, with hipbone
   removed and excess fat trimmed
¼ cup fresh lemon juice
2 tablespoons fresh rosemary,
   finely minced

1 tablespoon ground black pepper
4 cloves garlic, cut into slivers
2 tablespoons olive oil

Mix the lemon juice, rosemary, and black pepper. Rub the wide end of the leg with ⅔ of the mixture.

Take a sharp-pointed knife, and cut 20 evenly-spaced slits in the roast (remember, this is not your weapon of choice so handle it carefully). Put a sliver of garlic in each slit.

Stir the olive oil into the remaining seasoning mixture. Re-rub the roast, especially around the slits. Use all of the seasoning mixture.

Position the roast, meaty side up, on a rack in a roasting pan. Place in the oven and immediately turn the temperature down to 325 degrees.

After about 1 ¼ hours check the temperature of the meat with an instant-read thermometer. Temperature should be 125 to 130 degrees for medium-rare or 135 to 145 degrees for medium. Meat must be cooked to at least 125 degrees to be thoroughly cooked, so if necessary leave it in for another 15 to 30 minutes. Once removed from the oven the roast does continue to cook and the temperature will increase about 5 degrees.

Remove from the oven. Place aluminum foil loosely over the roast and let sit for about 15 minutes.

This roast is flavorful as is, but can be served with traditional mint sauce...or for a new spin on an old favorite, try a red onion confit or mango chutney.

Serves 6 to 8

Stuffed Peppers

JANE HADDAM

$\mathscr{I}$ invented this recipe to prove that I was a better cook than my mother. Seriously. For a while there, I was interested in being a better everything than my mother, sort of as a matter of principle. I managed the cooking, I think. And she doesn't write. On the other hand, I rather think that at this late date, I'm never going to turn myself into a coloratura soprano.

My mother is now very old, and very ill, and needs nursing care around the clock. Sometimes she won't eat, and they get afraid she's going to starve from lack of interest in food.

But she'll always eat this, if I make it and bring it along.

8 large bell peppers	2 teaspoons honey
3 tablespoons butter	1 to 2 tablespoons cinnamon
1 medium onion, coarse chopped	3 chicken bullion cubes, dissolved in
10 ounces white mushrooms,	3 cups water *or* 3 cups chicken broth
trimmed and sliced	2 pounds ground beef
½ cup raisins	Garlic powder to taste
½ cup pine nuts	1 bottle good tomato juice
1 ½ cups cooked long-grain rice	

Cut the very tops off the bell peppers and discard. Clean the seeds and veins out of the insides of the peppers; set peppers aside. Preheat the oven to 350 degrees. Melt the butter in a saucepan. Sauté the onions and mushrooms in the butter until soft. Add the raisins, pine nuts, rice, honey, and cinnamon. Add the water with bullion cubes or chicken broth, and bring to a boil. Cover and reduce heat to low.

Important: You should check on the rice mixture while making this recipe. Rice is done when water is absorbed, usually about 15 minutes. Put the ground beef and garlic in a frying pan, and cook together until the meat is done, running a fork through meat to break it up into small pieces. Fill a good-sized pot half full with water and bring to a boil. Quickly parboil each of the trimmed peppers for 2 to 3 minutes. Put the peppers into a casserole dish, open tops up.

Combine the meat with the rice in a large bowl. Fill each pepper with the mixture. If there is mixture left over, stuff it around the peppers, or eat it straight. Pour the tomato juice over the peppers, covering the tops but not filling the casserole. Cover the casserole with aluminum foil or its own cover, and place in a preheated oven for 1 hour.

Gregor Demarkian, retired head of the FBI's Behavioral Science Unit, appears in Jane Haddam's mysteries, including *Somebody Else's Music*, *True Believers* and *Skeleton Key*. She has been nominated for the Edgar three times and the Anthony once, prompting her to comment, "Always a bridesmaid...."

Glasgow Inn Beef Stew
STEVE HAMILTON

Served weekly at the Glasgow Inn in Paradise, Michigan—Alex McKnight's favorite hangout—this recipe is the specialty of the owner, Jackie Connery.

    Vegetable oil for browning beef
    1 medium onion, coarsely chopped
    6 or 7 cloves garlic, minced
    3 pounds stew beef (such as rump or round), cut into large cubes
    Flour for dredging beef
    8 or 9 carrots, peeled and cut into large pieces
    7 or 8 potatoes, peeled and cut into large pieces
    1 16-ounce bag frozen pearl (small) onions
    1 bottle beer*
    Approximately ⅓ cup flour
    Salt and pepper to taste

Preheat oven to 300 degrees. Heat the oil in a large Dutch oven or other oven-safe pot. Brown the onion and garlic. Dredge the beef in flour seasoned with salt and pepper, add to the pot, and cook over high heat until browned. Lower the heat and add the carrots, potatoes, and pearl onions. Add the beer, flour (use less for a thinner sauce), and salt and pepper to taste. Mix well. Cover and place in the oven. Simmer slowly for several hours until the meat and vegetables are tender.

Serve in bowls, and top with ketchup (as Alex prefers) if you really want to drive Jackie crazy....

*Ideally, this beer is produced and purchased in Canada, with many more bottles left over to serve with the stew!

Steve Hamilton's Alex McKnight series, all set in Michigan's Upper Peninsula, began with the Edgar-winning *A Cold Day In Paradise* and continues with the fifth book in the series, *Blood Is The Sky*. His website is found at www.authorstevehamilton.com.

Jessie Arnold's Drunk Pot Roast

SUE HENRY

When my editor, Tom Colgan, left Morrow/Avon after editing my second two books he requested one thing as a parting gift: the recipe for Jessie Arnold's Drunk Pot Roast that is mentioned in my third book, *Sleeping Lady*. Since then I have been asked for this recipe by numerous readers and fans, so I think it is only fitting that it be included in *A Second Helping of Murder*.

Jessie's friend and lover, Alex Jensen, is a huge fan of this particular menu item. In fact: *Jessie's drunk roasts, simmered for hours in Killian's Red Lager and carefully selected herbs, came close to eliciting genuflection from Alex....Glad to be home, he closed his eyes and appreciatively breathed in deeply the scent of the roast.* (from *Sleeping Lady*). Because of the yeast in lager, as it roasts, this recipe fills the house with an irresistible scent reminiscent of baking bread.

> 2 to 3 pounds chuck roast of beef
> (moose may be substituted if you live in Alaska)
> ¼ cup canola oil
> Salt and freshly ground pepper to taste
> 2 large onions, quartered
> 2 cloves garlic, crushed
> 1 stalk celery, with leaves, quartered
> 2 bottles Killian's Red Lager
> A sprig each: fresh rosemary, basil, and marjoram, if possible (otherwise add a
> pinch of each in dry form) to taste
> Beef stock or broth (as needed)
> Potatoes, peeled, if you like, halved or quartered if large (optional)
> Carrots, peeled or scraped (optional)

Preheat the oven to 325 degrees. In a large skillet, heat the oil. Sear the beef on all sides over medium high heat. Drain off all but a tablespoon of excess oil. Season the beef with salt and pepper, and place in a large roasting pan. Add the onion, garlic, and celery to the skillet and sauté until the onions are golden, about 5 minutes, on medium heat. Pour 2 bottles of Killian's Red Lager over the onions, garlic, and celery. Add the rosemary, basil, and marjoram, fresh or dry, and heat to a simmer. Pour the contents of the skillet over the beef in the roasting pan. Cover and roast slowly for 3 to 4 hours in the center of the oven, checking periodically to be sure the roasting pan does not go dry. If more liquid is needed use beef stock or broth (or more Killian's), heated before adding. (Warning: moose, a leaner meat, may take longer to roast.) During the last hour of roasting you may add carrots and potatoes, if desired.

Remove the roast from the oven. Remove the meat and vegetables from the roasting pan, and any excess fat from the juices in the pan. Thicken the remaining pan juices with flour, adding beef stock or broth if needed for the desired consistency.

Alex is usually in charge of making biscuits to accompany Jessie's Drunk Pot Roast. His personal recipe: Search the pantry to find the box of Bisquick and follow the instructions on the label. "Those who live in southern states and have a biscuit-making reputation to uphold should use their own recipe," says Alex.

Serve roast immediately…with biscuits of course!

Makes approximately 4 to 6 servings, but leftovers make great sandwiches.

Sue Henry is author of the Alaskan Jessie Arnold/Alex Jensen series, *Murder on the Iditarod Trail* through *Death Trap*. She is working on a new Maxie and Stretch series, the first of which is *The Serpents Trail*.

Machaca

DIANA GABALDON

*H*ere's a recipe that will work for Atkins' followers or low-fat devotees—though I'm afraid there really isn't a good vegetarian equivalent. Developed by Mexican peasants faced with the prospect of eating elderly goat, stringy rabbit, or the leftover remnants of the village cow, machaca is a way of rendering any cut of meat both edible and tasty. That being so, it really doesn't matter what cut you select, or how big it is, but I usually buy a large rump roast, because it's not very fatty, and is easy to clean. By and large, a pound of raw beef will yield about 10 to 12 ounces of machaca.

> A large chunk of beef, any cut (one pound will probably feed 2-3 people)*
> 1 onion, any color (yellow Spanish onion is traditional)
> 1 green bell pepper
> 1 red bell pepper
> 1 head of garlic
> Cilantro, chopped (optional)
> Salt and pepper to taste

***Note:** Traditional Mexican cookery occasionally uses *carne seca*—dried beef, or jerky—instead of fresh beef. In this case, you don't need to boil or shred it, but will need to allow a longer steaming time. (Note: don't use spiced jerky, if you employ this option.)

Preparation has several steps; this isn't a recipe for people rushing home from work and wondering what to microwave. On the other hand, once made, machaca will keep—and improve in flavor—for up to a week in the refrigerator, and can be used in a number of different quick, tasty dishes.

Boil the beef. This is simple; it just takes awhile. Put the raw beef in a large pot, cover it with water, and put over a medium-high flame. Bring to a boil, and keep gently boiling for 3 to 5 hours. The only thing to remember is to check the pot and add more water, to prevent the meat boiling dry. You know it's done when you stick a fork in the meat and it begins to fall apart.

Chill. Scoop the beef out of the water, put it in a large bowl, cover, and put in the refrigerator to chill. Overnight is best, but 2 or 3 hours will do.

Shred the chilled, boiled beef with your fingers, removing any gristle or fat. Put shredded beef in a large frying pan or stewing pan—any wide, shallow pan with a lid (or that can be covered with a sheet of aluminum foil).

Add the vegetables and spices. The thing to observe here is that the vegetables are spice in this dish. Ergo, you don't want to have big chunks of garlic, onion, and peppers—you want to use quantities of very finely minced vegetable, which will dessicate in the cooking and flavor the meat. How much? Depends how much you like garlic, essentially. For a 4-to-6-pound roast, I'd use a whole head of garlic, myself. Mince a quantity of onion equivalent to the quantity of garlic, and an equal quantity each of red and green peppers. If you like cilantro (aka coriander leaf) and can get it fresh, add 2 or 3 tablespoonfuls, also minced. Mix all the minced vegetables into the shredded beef, adding a light sprinkle of salt and pepper.

Steam. Pour a small amount of water over the meat and vegetables—3 or 4 tablespoonfuls. The water is to keep the cooking meat from sticking to the pot, and gently steam it, not to braise or stew it, so you don't need a lot. Cover the pan and set over a low heat. This is a good dish to make while you're doing something else time-consuming in or near the kitchen, because while you don't need to do anything but stir it occasionally, and now and then add more water, you *do* need to keep an eye on it. Check every 5 to 10 minutes, stirring the meat, adding water as needed, if the meat begins to dry or stick. Add additional salt or pepper, as desired, when stirring. Continue this process until all the vegetables are desiccated—appearing as no more than colorful shreds among the meat—and the meat is uniformly moist and totally shredded. This usually takes 30 to 45 minutes.

A version of this dish in Cuban cuisine is known as *ropas viejas*—"old clothes"—which will tell you something about what it looks like when done. Machaca can be served as a main dish, accompanied by fresh salsa, fried plantains, or fried potatoes, rice and beans (traditional Mexican-style Pinto beans—whole or refried—or Cuban black beans), or eggs. It also makes a delicious filling for tacos, flautas, enchiladas, tostadas, or burritos—my favorite is a machaca burrito, made by ladling a couple of large spoonfuls of machaca into the center of a flour tortilla, covering with grated cheddar cheese, and sticking in the microwave for 30 seconds (just enough to melt the cheese). Top with chunky tomato salsa (fruit salsas are also great), wrap the tortilla, and eat!

Machaca is time-consuming, but remarkably simple to cook—and since the flavor will improve even more as the pepper-onion-garlic flavors continue to blend, it's great to make a big batch to keep in the refrigerator—ideal for Atkins'-approved snacking!

Diana Gabaldon's *New York Times* best-selling *Outlander* series, including *The Fiery Cross* and *Drums of Autumn,* features Major Lord John, who also appears in her new trilogy beginning with *Lord John and the Private Matters.*

Peppered Steak

DOLORES JOHNSON

*A*ny dish that's flambéed comes under the category of what I consider "fun food." (In the book I'm currently working on, tentatively titled *Taking the Wrap*, look for Mandy's employee, Betty the Bag Lady, to have an unexpected reaction to cherries jubilee when it's set afire at her table.)

The only recipe I ever created (without following instructions in a cookbook) was developed after my husband and I lived in Tunisia. We'd occasionally go to a French restaurant where I'd watch the chef prepare peppered steak at our table. When we came home, I came up with my own version of the dish.

> 1-inch-thick sirloin or filet mignon steaks (enough for four people)
> Peppercorn to taste
> Salt
> 4 tablespoons butter
> 2 teaspoons Worcestershire sauce
> 2 tablespoons catsup
> 2 teaspoons mustard
> Brandy or cognac

Crush the peppercorns coarsely in a pan using a mallet (do not grind). Press into both sides of the steaks. Sprinkle the bottom of frying pans with salt (a teaspoon per pan). When the salt begins to brown, put the steaks in the pans uncovered over high heat. Reduce to medium and cook to the desired degree of doneness.

In a separate pan, melt the butter and add the Worcestershire sauce, catsup, and mustard. When heated, pour the sauce over the steaks in the frying pans, and flambé the steaks with 1 jigger of brandy or cognac per serving (or a little less).

Dolores Johnson is the author of the Mandy Dyer series, which includes *A Dress to Die For*, *Homicide and Old Lace*, and *Buttons and Foes*.

Grilled Beef Tenderloin with Madeira Mushroom Sauce
M. DIANE VOGT

This recipe reputedly was enjoyed during Thomas Jefferson's time. The ingredients are certainly classic enough. Whether it's true or not, I've served this dish to many a guest and never had one complaint! This recipe is suitable for a five-pound beef tenderloin or a seven-pound prime rib.

Bon Appetit!

One hour before roasting, rub the beef with the following mixture and allow to stand at room temperature.

> 2 tablespoons chutney (I use London Pub, Major Grey Chutney, made with
>   mangoes, but there are several brands on the market)
> 1/4 teaspoon fresh ground pepper
> 1/2 teaspoon dried mustard
> 2 tablespoons melted butter
> 1/2 teaspoon salt

Roast the rubbed beef in an open roasting pan at the appropriate temperature until desired doneness. Be sure to preheat the oven. (As an example, prime rib should be seared at 450 degrees for 10 minutes, then roasted at 250 degrees for 25 minutes per pound for medium rare; beef tenderloin should be roasted at 450 degrees for 55 minutes for medium rare.) Prime rib should be roasted rib side down. If you choose to use the tenderloin, get flat beef bones at the butcher and place the meat on the bones for roasting. This is a very lean cut of beef and it will not produce enough drippings for the sauce without the beef bones. The tenderloin should not touch the metal in the pan while cooking.

Remove the beef from the pan, and transfer to warm platter. Keep warm while making the sauce. The sauce is made in the roasting pan on top of the stove. Brown the pan drippings. If there is not enough fat, add 2 tablespoons of butter. Add:

> 1 cup sliced fresh mushrooms
> 1/2 cup beef consommé

Cook until the mushrooms are the desired doneness. Just before serving, add 1 tablespoon Madeira wine, and cook for 30 seconds to 1 minute.

More sauce can be made by increasing all of the sauce ingredients.

M. Diane Vogt is the author of four books in the acclaimed Judge Wilhelmina Carson legal suspense series set in Tampa. Judge Carson lives above a five-star restaurant that serves heavenly food like this recipe, reportedly enjoyed by Thomas Jefferson. Her latest is *Six Bills*. Visit her website at www.mdianevogt.com.

Bel Barrett's Brisket

JANE ISENBERG

This recipe saved my life. Several years ago, my daughter Rachel and her friend Mike decided to co-host a Passover Seder in the Seattle suburbs. Mike's mother Mimi and I turned out to be the only Jews on the lengthy guest list. Mimi couldn't make it there from Chicago, and Rachel e-mailed me that she hoped I'd come a day or two early and "do the brisket." I panicked. My brisket, concocted from memory and desire rather than a recipe, was unreliable, sometimes tender and savory, yes. But I have to confess that every once in a while it emerged from the oven with all the appeal of a shoe boiled in vinegar. So I found a recipe in a Passover cookbook and put my own twist on it. It was a big hit and saved my reputation as a Jewish mother.

Like many midlife women, Bel Barrett, the protagonist of my series, usually prefers dialing for dinner or frequenting one of Hoboken's many ethnic eateries to cooking. She's been there and done that, thank you very much. But occasionally Bel, or her mother Sadie, or her partner Sol makes a holiday meal. And when the holiday's a Jewish one, they make brisket. When I write those scenes, this is the recipe I envision them using. It's foolproof, fast, and the results are delicious. If there are any leftovers, they are wonderful too. Near the beginning of *Out of Hormone's Way*, the fifth book in the series, Bel and Sol chow down on brisket left over from their Seder. After I wrote that scene, I found an excuse to make brisket. It's that good.

3 pounds, first cut brisket	1 small or medium onion, sliced
1 cup chile sauce	3 whole cloves
½ cup brown sugar	6 whole black peppercorns
¼ cup dry red wine	3 bay leaves
¼ cup water	

Preheat the oven to 325 degrees. Rinse the brisket. In a small bowl, combine the chile sauce, brown sugar, wine, and water, and mix. Pour ¼ of this mixture into a roasting pan. Place the brisket, fat side up, on the sauce, and distribute the onion, cloves, peppercorns, and bay leaves over the meat. Top with the remaining chile sauce mixture. Cover tightly (I use heavy-duty foil) and bake 50 to 55 minutes per pound, until the meat is fork tender.

Remove from the oven and take out the bay leaves, cloves, and peppercorns. I puree the onions and gravy in the blender. Refrigerate the meat and gravy separately. When you are ready to use, slice the meat against the grain, and arrange it in an oil-sprayed roasting pan. Pour on the sauce, cover, and heat at 375 degrees for about 30 minutes.

Jane Isenberg's series featuring the menopausal Bel Barrett includes *The "M" Word*, *Death in a Hot Flash*, and *Midlife Can Be Murder*.

Christmas Eve Cholent
IRENE MARCUSE

Although the very name of this recipe seems like an oxymoron—cholent, after all, is a traditional Jewish Sabbath meal, prepared on Friday afternoon and left in the back of a lit oven to cook slowly over night, ready for a Saturday meal—Christmas Eve Cholent is the perfect synthesis of religions in Anita Servi's household, as it is in mine. In *Consider the Alternative*, Anita herself says:

> *"We do all the holidays, eight nights of Chanukah, six nights for Kwanzaa, the big enchilada of Christmas in between… The holiday observance that's all our own is an annual Christmas Eve party, attended by a mix of stray Jews and various other friends close enough to be family. I make Benno's mother's cholent, a Sabbath dish that's become a party tradition, and everyone else brings whatever they want."*

1 pound dried great northern beans
¼ cup vegetable oil
2 large onions, chopped
3 shallots, chopped
4 cloves garlic, chopped
2 ½ pounds boneless flanken or brisket, cut in 2-inch chunks
½ pound pastrami (buy whole and cut into cubes)
1 tablespoon Hungarian sweet paprika
1 tablespoon honey
½ cup pearl barley
Salt and pepper to taste

Soak the beans in water, covered to 2 inches above, for 4 hours to overnight.

Put 6 cups of water on to boil. Meanwhile, heat the oil, and sauté the onions and shallots until golden. Add garlic for 1 minute. Remove the vegetables from the pot, and set aside. Brown the beef and remove from the pot. Brown the pastrami, then add paprika and honey. Return the onions and meat to the pot, then stir in the barley. Drain the beans and add to the pot.

Add the boiling water. Bake covered at 400 degrees for 30 minutes. Season with salt and pepper, then cover the pot with foil and lid. Turn the oven down to 225 degrees and bake at least 7 or 8 hours, or overnight

Can be served over rice. Feeds 8 to 10.

Set on the "upper left side" of Manhattan, Irene Marcuse's Anita Servi mystery series features a social worker who helps those who cannot find help elsewhere cope with living in a city that can't always afford to provide what they need. Titles include *The Death of an Amiable Child, Guilty Mind*, and *Consider the Alternative*. Learn more at www.marcuse.org/irene.

Golbki

(Addy McNeil's Favorite Stuffed Cabbage Leaves)

JAN BROGAN

*M*y protagonist Addy McNeil is a hardworking journalist with hardly any time to eat, let alone cook, but on occasion she goes home to her parent's house in Worcester, Massachusetts, where her mother forces her to eat a decent meal. In *A Confidential Source*, Addy has moved from Boston to Providence, which is even closer to Worcester. In one scene, her mother, Edie McNeil, tries to woo her daughter to come back to the house and stay another night by promising to make Addy's favorite stuffed cabbage leaves. It is testament to the insanity of Addy's life (and the heat of the murder investigation) that Addy never gets to come back and have her favorite dish.

Don't make the same mistake!

1 head of cabbage	1 16-ounce can of ground, peeled tomatoes
1 ½ cups ground pork or beef or turkey or combination	4 chopped scallions
1 ½ cup cooked rice	2 teaspoons fresh lemon juice
3 tablespoons caraway seeds	1 scant teaspoon thyme
2 tablespoons horseradish	Salt and pepper to taste
	½ cup water

It makes it a lot easier if you start by removing the core from the head of cabbage. Scald the cabbage in a large pot of boiling water. Leaves will begin to loosen and are easy to pry off one or two at a time. As they wilt, remove them from the pot, and put on a plate to cool before using.

In a separate bowl, mix the ground meat, rice, caraway seeds, horseradish, and a pinch of salt. Spoon the mixture into a base of cabbage leaf, fold over the two opposite sides, and roll toward the top of leaf. Put the folded side down in a large baking dish. After the filling is used up, add extra leaves on top. Combine the ground tomato, scallions, lemon, and thyme. Salt and pepper to taste. Pour over the cabbage leaves into the dish. Pour the water into the corners of the baking dish, and cover tightly with foil.

Bake at 375 degrees for half an hour. Uncover and lower the temperature to 300 degrees and cook for an hour longer.

Best served with thick rye bread or sourdough bread.

Makes about 15 to 18 stuffed cabbage leaves.

Jan Brogan is the author of *Final Copy*, named one of the best eight novels of 2001 by *The Drood Review of Mystery*, and *A Confidential Source*. Visit Jan's website, www.JanBrogan.com.

James Callahan's Murderous Meatloaf
AL BLANCHARD

*B*oston Homicide Detective James Callahan does much of the cooking for his family, a real trick because he only knows how to prepare two meals. About this meatloaf, his friend B.J. said, "I refuse to eat anything that can be used to shingle a roof if there's any left over." I like it, and so does my dog Asher.

          1 cup soft bread crumbs
          1 cup milk
          1 ½ pounds ground beef
          1 egg
          ¼ teaspoon pepper
          1 teaspoon Worcestershire sauce
          2 tablespoons minced onions
          ½ cup ketchup
          3 tablespoons brown sugar
          1 tablespoon prepared mustard
          ¼ tablespoon salt
          ½ cup water

Add the bread crumbs to the milk, and let stand for a few minutes. Mix with the ground beef, egg, pepper, Worcestershire Sauce, and onion. Shape into a loaf, and put in a baking pan. Combine the ketchup, brown sugar, mustard, salt, and water, and pour over the meatloaf. Bake at 300 degrees for 1 hour and 15 minutes. Baste occasionally.

Makes 6 to 8 servings.

Al Blanchard is the creator of two mystery series, one featuring James Callahan and the other school teacher Steve Asher. His titles include *Murder at Walden Pond, The Iscariot Conspiracy* and *The Disappearance of Jenna Drago*. His website can be found at www.alblanchard.com.

Stuffed Flank Steak

BILL STACKHOUSE

*O*ne lump-sum divorce settlement from Stevie Henderson, added to a life's savings from her brother Porky Jarvis, a retired Air Force Master Sergeant, combined with a general store for sale in the Catskills and the expertise of a talented building contractor, resulted in The Plough & Whistle, the finest English Pub this side of the Atlantic. Patrons drive from as far as Saugerties and New Paltz to soak up the warm, cheery atmosphere and indulge themselves with the culinary dinner creations from the pudgy pubkeeper of Peekamoose Heights.

"Two Moroccan hens and one stuffed flank steak," Porky Jarvis called out as he entered behind the bar from the doorway to the grille, carrying three steaming plates and a basket of rolls on a large wooden tray. Now in his fifties, with a head as bald as a cue-ball and with a much-rounder body than ever—in addition to still being short and having little ears—his nickname had become even more apropos.

The trio at the bar turned to him with a mixture of umms and ahhs.

"Smells delicious, Porky," the youngest member of the threesome observed as she leaned her elbows on the upper brass rail of the bar, cradled her face in her hands, and deeply inhaled the aroma of the food. Batting her eyelashes at the portly bartender, she said, "Are you sure you won't consider marrying me?"

—from *Encore To Murder: An Ed McAvoy Mystery*

6 tablespoons unsalted butter
¼ cup sweet onion, minced
½ tablespoon minced garlic
¼ cup olive oil
2 cups Crimini mushrooms, diced into ½ inch pieces
1 cup Portabello mushrooms, diced into ½ inch pieces
1 tablespoon chopped parsley
½ teaspoon chopped oregano
½ teaspoon rosemary, crushed
½ tablespoon coarse ground black pepper
2 tablespoons Worcestershire sauce
¼ cup white wine
6 ounces Feta cheese, crumbled
2-pound flank steak
6 slices Lebanon bologna
6 slices Provolone cheese
(Cooking twine)

In a large frying pan, sauté the onions and garlic in the butter and 1 tablespoon of olive oil on medium-high heat until the onions are translucent. Add the mushrooms, and sauté for 2 minutes. Stir in the parsley, oregano, rosemary, and black pepper. Stir in the Worcestershire and wine. Bring the mixture to a boil. Reduce heat to medium-low and simmer for 5 minutes, stirring occasionally.

Preheat the oven to 350 degrees. In a bowl, combine the mushroom mixture with the Feta cheese.

Pound out the flank steak between 2 layers of plastic wrap until it is approximately ⅜-inch thick. (If you have the butcher run it once through the cuber, it will be easier to pound out. Don't let him run it through twice like he does for cubed steak, or you'll end up with dog food after you pound it out.)

Place the bologna slices on top of the flank steak. Place Provolone slices on top of the bologna. Spread the mushroom/Feta mixture on top of the Provolone slices. Roll up the flank steak and tie with cooking twine in 4 or 5 places.

In a skillet, sear the stuffed flank steak in the remainder of the olive oil, turning it as necessary. Place the seared stuffed flank steak on an aluminum-foil-covered cookie sheet and bake at 350 degrees for 45 minutes. Let rest for 10 minutes. Slice on the diagonal and serve.

Bill Stackhouse's mysteries featuring Detroit homicide cop-turned small town Catskills police chief Ed McAvoy include *Encore to Murder* and *Stream of Death*. Learn more at www.billstackhouse.com.

Meat Pasty

JOHN MACKIE

It was only a ten minute walk to Maureen's place, and he pondered whether it had been a subconscious desire to see her, or his lust for pasty, that had motivated him to accept her Christmas Day dinner invitation. It was, he tried assuring himself, the lure of pasty. Meat pasties were either Scottish or Cornish in origin; Savage had never found out, for sure, which. All he knew was the simple recipe went back generations on his father's side, to Nanny Nye, his feisty Scottish great-grandmother who had operated a prize-fighter's training gym near Coney Island back in the teens and twenties. She was a rip, he'd been told, every bit as tough as the questionable mugs who hung out there. Pasties were nothing more than cubed pieces of round steak draped over a mound of diced potato and topped with a strip of suet. Wrapped in a pie crust, the ingredients were baked until the beef juices seeped down through the potatoes and caramelized into the bottom crust. When made softball size, they were a filling energy supplier for Highlander husbands who toted them around in their coat pockets until the lunch whistle blew. When made half a football size, it was a dinner feast. They were, for some, an acquired taste. Too dry, many would say. Thorn Savage had been raised on them; to him they were manna from heaven. And, best of all, they contained no veggies. He hated veggies; never ate them.

—from *East Side*

$\mathcal{P}$asty is basically a meat and potato pie. It is a dish popular throughout the British Isles. Many believe it to have originated in Cornwall, England, and it is therefore often referred to as Cornish pasty. Though it has many variations, based on personal choice of ingredients, the recipe below is for a basic pasty—Thorn Savage's favorite.

Pastry

Pasty is not made with a fragile or puff pastry. Therefore, a standard dessert pie crust is exactly the right consistency. Pillsbury or Betty Crocker box mixes are what we generally use. 1 box makes 2 casings. For the purist, however, here's how to make your own:

> 2 cups sifted all-purpose flour
> 1 tablespoon salt
> ⅔ cup shortening
> 5 to 6 tablespoons cold water

Mix the ingredients and shape the dough into a ball. Refrigerate for 10 minutes. Cut the ball in half and roll out 2 pasty casings on a floured board.

Pasty Filling

> Round steak, cubed (approximately ½ pound)
> 1 to 2 medium uncooked potatoes, diced or sliced
> A small strip of suet
> Salt and pepper to taste
> 1 egg, beaten

Prepare the pastry dough for one pie crust. Roll out the dough on a floured board into a circle the size of a dinner plate. Mound the cubed steak and sliced potato in the center of dough; place the strip of suet at top of the mound. Salt and pepper to taste. Fold the dough over the mound, creating a half-circle. Cut away any excess dough and crimp along the edges with a fork to seal. Before cooking, ventilate for steam release with fork holes in the top of pasty. Brush the pasty with beaten egg for golden glaze.

Put the pasty on a greased cookie sheet. Cook at 350 degrees for 90 minutes. The pasty is done when juices from the beef have seeped down through the potatoes and caramelized into the bottom crust.

Optional Filling Ingredients: Onion, turnip, other vegetables, whatever.

John Mackie's novels about NYPD sergeant Thornton Savage include *East Side*, *Manhattan South* and *Manhattan North*.

Aunt Maggie's Three-Secret Steak and Kidney Pudding

PIP GRANGER

According to young Rosie, Auntie Maggie made the best steak and kidney pudding in the whole world and the punters at the Old Compton Street café that nestled in 1950s Soho were inclined to agree. There's a few secrets to her recipe which up until now have never been revealed.

The first secret is that Auntie Maggie always cooked her steak and kidney separately as a stew before she turned it into a pudding.

For the filling, you will need:

> 1 pound stewing steak
> ½ pound kidney, preferably lamb
> 2 level teaspoons plain white flour, seasoned with salt and pepper to taste
> 1 large onion, chopped
> Water
> Bay leaf and thyme, dried or fresh to taste
> Oil or a small knob of butter

First, prepare the meat by cutting it into bite-size chunks, removing the skin and core from the kidneys (or ask your butcher to do it). Coat the meat with seasoned flour. Sweat the onion in a little oil or fat in a stew pan. Add the meat and toss lightly until sealed. Add the bay leaf, thyme, and enough water to ensure the meat is covered. Put a lid on the pan and simmer gently for at least 2 hours, checking now and then to see whether more water is required to prevent sticking and burning. Once cooked, set aside.

For the pudding you will need:

> 7 ounces self-raising flour
> ½ level teaspoon salt
> 3 ½ ounces shredded beef suet
> Mustard powder to taste*
> Approximately 7 tablespoons cold water

Mix together the flour, suet, mustard powder, and salt in a bowl, then add enough water to give a light, elastic dough. Knead very gently until smooth. Roll out on a floured board until approx ¼-inch thick.

*Auntie Maggie's second secret was that she added dried mustard powder to her flour and suet before adding water to gave the pudding an extra "zing," but don't overdo it. Another option is to add dried thyme to the dough instead of to the stew.

Making the pudding:
Grease a 1 ½- or 2-pint pudding basin, then line it with about three quarters of the suet-crust pastry, saving the rest for the lid.

Spoon the steak-and-kidney mixture into the lined bowl. Add just a little water if the mixture looks dry. Roll out the pastry to make the lid; dampen the edge and then place on top of the meat, making sure to seal the edges of the pastry well.

Traditionally, the pudding basin would then be wrapped in a clean, cotton cloth, tied firmly with string (allowing a loop left over to help you lift the hot basin when the pudding is cooked). However, wrapping the basin in aluminum foil or greaseproof paper will do just as well.

Half-fill a large saucepan or a steamer with water. Place the pudding basin inside, cover, and simmer for 1 ½ to 2 hours.

Serve with lightly steamed vegetables.

Auntie Maggie's third secret is also optional. She would make her own stock from carrots, onions, celery, a few peppercorns, a sprig or two of parsley, and some beef bones, and simmer it for some hours before adding it to the stew mix instead of the water. If beef bones are not available, a vegetable stock simmered for just half-an-hour will do very well. Left-over stock may be put into ice cube trays and frozen for future use.

Pip Granger's mysteries set in 1950s Soho are *Not All Tarts Are Apple* and *The Widow Ginger.*

Jean's Shepherd's Pie

FRED HUNTER

*A*lex Reynolds is a former graphic artist who found himself working for the CIA after a chance encounter in a bar landed him in the center of a deadly foreign plot. Along with his British mother, Jean, who was happy to have their peaceful existence interrupted by what she terms "a spot of espionage," and his lover, Peter Livesay, Alex continues his part-time status as an agent, the three of them often finding themselves involved in complicated and dangerous spy plots. In their most recent outing, *The Chicken Asylum*, the family shelters a defecting Iraqi soldier, who delights in his first taste of their favorite dish, Shepherd's Pie.

6 large russet potatoes
2 tablespoons butter
Milk
1 pound lean ground beef
1 onion, finely chopped
1 carrot, finely chopped
2 teaspoons flour
"A little bit" of gravy browning (optional)
Salt and pepper

To prepare the mashed potatoes: Cook the potatoes in boiling salted water until tender, about 20 minutes. Drain the potatoes and mash, adding 2 tablespoons of butter, and enough milk to form a firm consistency.

For the meat base: Bring 1 cup of water to a boil. Add the beef, onion, and carrot, and a bit of salt and pepper. Cook on a medium heat for about 40 minutes, stirring occasionally. Water may be added to keep the mixture moist but not soggy. In a small bowl, combine 2 teaspoons of flour and a bit of gravy browning. Stir in water until the mixture becomes a thick paste, then add to the meat mixture a few minutes before removing it from the stove to thicken it. Transfer the meat mixture to an ovenproof dish, covering the inside of the dish like a pie-crust shell. Cover the meat with the mashed potatoes, score the top of the potatoes with a fork, then place under a broiler just long enough to brown the top. You're in for a treat!

Fred Hunter's books include *The Chicken Asylum*, *National Nancy* and in his other series, *The Mummy's Ransom* and *Ransom for a Killing*. His website can be found at http://home.earthlink.net/~fhunter.

Teleci* Fenimore

ROBIN HATHAWAY

*D*r. Andrew Fenimore is a Philadelphia cardiologist whose mother was Czech. The subplot of *The Doctor Dines In Prague* concerns Fenimore's search for a bona fide Czech meal, complete with schnitzel, dumplings and palacinky. Because Fenimore is busy solving a mystery, he never has time for anything but pizza and burgers from McDonalds. The irony is, it is not until Fenimore returns to Philadelphia, that he finally has a Czech dinner, prepared by his Czech cousin, who buys all the ingredients at the famous Reading Terminal, where the Amish farmers sell their wares.

> 2 ½ pound veal cutlets
> ¼ pound butter
> 15 medium mushroom caps, chopped
> 1 dozen asparagus spears
> 4 brown eggs (for deeper color)
> ¼ cup chopped chives
> ⅛ cup whole milk
> ¼ teaspoon salt
> ¼ teaspoon pepper
> 2 Czech china plates

Cook the cutlets with ⅛ pound butter in a saucepan until the proper color brown (not too light, not too dark.) Keep warm in a double boiler. Add the gravy from the pan to the double boiler. Sauté the mushrooms in a separate pan with ⅛ pound butter. Boil the asparagus until tender. Beat the eggs, and add mushrooms, chives, milk, salt and pepper. Scramble to perfection. (Not too fluffy, not too damp.)

Warm the plates in the oven at 150 degrees. Serve the cutlets, topped with the egg/mushroom mixture, and garnished with asparagus on warm Czech plates. Accompany with a dry white wine.

* Czech for veal

This recipe is from one of Dr. Fenimore's early appearances in Robin Hathaway's *The Doctor and The Dead Man's Chest*. Fenimore's most recent adventure takes place in *The Doctor Dines in Prague*.

Kill It (or Skillet) of Porc Normande
GRAHAM R. WOOD

As my detective serves manfully in the great and constant French battle to rid himself of even the last vestiges of the devil hunger, I thought that you might be interested in the recipe for one of the meals featured in the books. This dish is drawn from Superintendent Lauriant's childhood roots in Normandy and Brittany. The dish is served to him by Jacques the Auvergnat in his café at Sarcelles sur Mures in "A Dead Man's Mourning," a story in *Death in Provence.*

Health Warning: Persons consuming Kill It of Porc Normande may experience certain side effects. These include:

1. Weight gain.
2. Higher cholesterol.
3. Increased risk of cardiac arrest.
4. A feeling of indolence and enhanced well being.
5. An increased fondness for French food.

To prepare: Invite five friends to your home and enjoy one or two aperitifs and each others' company. Lay a good table. Open the wine.

For the Main Dish

1 tablespoon oil
1 tablespoon butter
6 pork chops or cutlets
2 medium onions
2 tart apples, peeled, cored and sliced
2 to 3 glasses Calvados (apple brandy), to taste
1 cup cider
Slightly less than 1 cup stock
2 tablespoons brown sugar
1 or 2 tablespoons ginger, to taste
Salt and pepper to taste
$\frac{1}{4}$ to $\frac{1}{3}$ cup cream

For Caramelized Apple Slices

2 tart apples, cored and sliced, but not peeled
2 tablespoons butter
2 tablespoons brown sugar

Heat the oil and butter in a skillet or shallow casserole. Trim the excess fat from the chops or cutlets, and brown them on both sides in hot oil and butter. Remove the pork, and add the onions to the skillet, and cook until soft—not brown. Add the apples, and cook over a high heat until both the apples and onions are golden brown.

In the meantime, blend the Calvados (apple brandy), cider, stock, brown sugar, and a little ginger.

Return the meat to the pan. Pour over a good measure of Calvados and flambé. Add the blended mixture plus salt and pepper, and bring to the boil. Cover and simmer for about 45 minutes or until the pork is tender when pierced, stirring or basting from time to time.

In the last few minutes, prepare the caramelized apples: Core and slice them, leaving on the skin. Heat the butter in a pan. Dip one side of each apple slice in brown sugar, and cook sugar side down in a pan over high heat until caramelized, about 4 or 5 minutes. Sprinkle on more sugar and turn the slices. Continue cooking, cover and keep warm.

Remove the pork from the skillet, and arrange on a large plate or serving dish. Bring the sauce to the boil and reduce if necessary. Add the cream, and bring back just to the boil and adjust seasoning. Spoon the sauce over the pork and garnish with the caramelized apple slices and with mixed leaves. Serve the remaining sauce separately in a sauceboat.

Accompaniments: To be served with fresh seasonal green vegetables, boiled or roast potatoes, and copious crusty French-style bread. The dish should also be accompanied by a bottle of Bordeaux (or a robust California red) and a large helping of good conversation.

To Follow: Camembert cheese, with the remaining wine, if any. If not, a second bottle is acceptable. Then, a glass of Calvados, plus good, strong coffee, and a read of a good mystery novel—preferably one of mine!

And, so to bed.

Graham R. Wood's mysteries, set in 1960s France, include *Detective Lauriant Investigates* and *Death in Provence*.

Campground Pork Chops à la Northern California
JANET LAPIERRE

When our daughters were small, our family, including a large dog, vacationed in an eight-foot cab-over camper on a Chevy pickup truck. Northern California has zillions of campgrounds, from fancy to primitive; we did near-primitive. The camper had a chemical toilet, a sink and water tank, a stove with oven, an icebox. There was room inside for bad-weather times. Otherwise, we lived outside and everyone but me (and the dog) slept outside. We also cooked outside, usually on the campground fireplace. Meals were based on canned stuff like tuna fish, chili, and spaghetti sauce. Often we added a pound of hamburger picked up in the nearest town when we broke camp to drive in for ice.

Near the end of one stay in a mountain campground, we learned that the nearby small town had a butcher shop famous for, of all things, pork. Suddenly everyone was weary of chili and pasta. We drove into town, bought a big batch of pork chops, returned to the campground and thought: now what? The following recipe, made with what we had on hand, was the result. We still use it at home. A less-specific version of this recipe is used in my sixth Port Silva Mystery, *Baby Mine*, by Cass, a sulky, disagreeable teenager who redeems herself in a campground setting by doing the one thing she does well and happily, cooking.

> 4 center-cut pork loin chops, boneless preferred
> Salt and pepper to taste
> Oil for frying
> 1 large or 2 medium onions, halved and sliced
> 2 or 3 apples, cored and sliced, not peeled
> 1 (at least) cup of white wine, preferably Chardonnay
>   or Sauvignon Blanc
> Rice or noodles, cooked

Cut the rim of fat from the chops and put it into a skillet over a medium-high flame. Salt and pepper the chops. When the fat has rendered out its oil, add vegetable oil, if needed, and brown the chops well on both sides. Remove and discard the bits of fat. Set the chops aside to keep warm. Put the onions in the pan, cover, and cook over a lower flame, stirring once or twice, until they have softened and picked up the brown residue from the chops. Arrange the chops on the onions. Lay the apple slices on and around the chops, and pour the white wine over all. Put the lid on the skillet, and cook at a gentle simmer until the chops are very tender and the apples very soft, about an hour. If necessary, add more white wine. (You may substitute chicken broth for white wine.) Serve with rice or noodles.

Leftovers may be roughly chopped and spread on a slice of sturdy bread like *pain au levain*, a bit of Dijon mustard optional.

Janet LaPierre's most recent books are *Baby Mine* and *Keepers*.

Frances' Felonious Sausage Casserole
EDIE CLAIRE

*L*eigh Koslow's idea of cooking may be microwaving a s'more, but that isn't her mother's fault. Frances tried for years to instill in her daughter a moral obligation to combine meat and vegetables at 350 degrees Fahrenheit, but alas, her efforts were for naught. Except for this zesty casserole, which is both tasty enough to please the younger set and easy enough that even Leigh can make it! It was, in fact, occupying the glass casserole dish that Frances nearly smashed over an intruder's head in *Never Preach Past Noon*. (Don't worry, the casserole escaped unscathed and rewarmed nicely.) Frances would like to state, however, that she does not consider either onions or mushrooms to be real vegetables, and that the fastidious cook should be sure to offer a side of peas.

> 1 pound sausage (the spicier the better)
> 3 cups cooked rice
> 1 cup chopped onion
> 1 can condensed cream of mushroom soup
> ½ to 1 cup shredded cheddar cheese

Brown the sausage; pour off the fat. Create layers of rice, sausage, onion, and soup in a casserole dish. Finish with a final round of rice, then top with cheese. Cover and bake at 350 degrees for 30 minutes.

You can follow the further adventures of Frances and her daughter in Edie Claire's *Never Kissed Goodnight* and *Never Tease a Siamese*.

$\mathcal{N}$O BONE TO PICK

Madame Yvette's Savory Leek Tart
RHYS BOWEN

*T*his recipe comes from *Evan and Elle*, the fourth in the Constable Evans Mystery series. Madame Yvette opens a French restaurant in a disused chapel and teaches the local ladies the art of French cooking. However, the local men are true to the maxim that "real men don't eat Quiche"—in spite of the fact that this is a scrumptuous recipe!

> 7 tablespoons cold butter
> 1 ¼ cups all purpose flour
> 3 tablespoons iced water

Cut the cold butter into pieces and rub into flour. When mixed it resembles breadcrumbs. Mix in the water to make dough. Roll out on a floured board. Line a 10-inch tart shell with pastry. Chill.

> 3 pounds leeks
> 4 tablespoons butter
> Salt and pepper to taste
> 3 eggs
> ½ cup heavy cream
> ½ cup Parmesan cheese
> ¼ cup Gruyere cheese
> Sun-dried tomatoes, cut into strips

Trim the roots and green off the leeks. Rinse and chop well.

Melt 4 tablespoons of butter in a skillet. Add the leeks, salt and pepper. Cook gently until soft.

Preheat the oven to 425 degrees. Whisk together the eggs, heavy cream, and ½ cup of Parmesan cheese. Add the leeks. Mix well. Pour into the unbaked tart shell. Sprinkle with ¼ cup of Gruyere (or Parmesan, if you prefer). Add strips of sun-dried tomato to decorate. Bake until well-browned, 30 to 40 minutes. Let cool 10 minutes before serving. Serve with mixed green salad.

Rhys Bowen's Constable Evans mysteries, set in contemporary Wales, include *Evans Above* and *Evan Only Knows*. The Molly Murphy mysteries, set in 1901 New York City, include *Murphy's Law* and *Death of Riley*. Her website is www.rhysbowen.com.

Tofu Lasagna
SANDRA LEVY CEREN

The protagonist of the Dr. Cory Cohen Mystery series is bi-racial. She is the daughter of a Japanese mother and an American father. Cory's love interest is an Italian. Here is my recipe for Tofu Lasagna, a somewhat unlikely combination of ingredients and the hit of many dinners.

> 1 large can tomato paste
> Fresh basil leaves, crumbled
> 3 cloves garlic, cut into tiny pieces
> Pinch of sugar
> Pinch of salt and pepper
> 1 pound lasagna, curly preferred for easy handling
> 1 teaspoon olive oil
> 1 tub soft tofu
> ¼ batch organic spinach, fresh or frozen (Note: if using frozen, toss in the microwave
>   for a minute or so; fresh can go straight from the bag.)
> Several thin slices mozzarella-style cheese

Place water to half way up a large pot, and set the pot to boil. In another pot, place the contents of one large can tomato paste, fill the can with water, basil, chopped garlic, sugar, salt, and pepper, and pour into the pot of tomato paste, and set it on low-medium heat.

Place the lasagna noodles, one at a time, into the boiling water with 1 teaspoon of olive oil. While the noodles cook, mash the tofu. When noodles are soft, drain. Lay out the lasagna noodles in a 12-by-9-by-2 ½-inch flat pan, alternating one layer of mashed tofu with one layer of spinach. Cover with the contents of the tomato paste mixture. You can dress the top layer with mozzarella cheese.

Place in an oven preheated to 350 degrees or so for approximately 45 minutes. Allow to cool for 5 to 10 minutes before serving.

Enjoy in good health!

Sandra Levy Ceren is the author of the Dr. Cory Cohen mystery novels *Prescription for Terror* and *Secrets from the Couch*.

Oliver Swithin's Curried Veggies
ALAN BEECHEY

$\mathcal{O}$liver Swithin, children's book author, is described in *An Embarrassment of Corpses* as *"an excellent practitioner of Indian cookery,"* who *"found the mere existence of anything as vague as curry powder depressing."* However, the only meal Oliver has made in the series so far is a banana and Brie sandwich, the outcome of a desperate lunchtime raid on a poorly stocked refrigerator. (Highly recommended incidentally: use pumpernickel or raisin bread, and if the cheese is runny enough, no other spread is necessary. Perhaps a sprinkling of alfalfa sprouts?)

The only character who actually prepares food in the books is Oliver's friend and housemate Susie Beamish. This is ironic, because it was widely thought that Susie could burn water. Oliver once found her looking for the instructions on a packet of cornflakes. But it isn't her culinary incompetence alone that causes every one of the theme restaurants she manages to go belly-up, because her loyal assistant chefs learned to bar her from the kitchen long ago. One of these failed enterprises—a snack bar on Baker Street serving food mentioned in the Sherlock Holmes novels—had a name that could be used for a later volume in this series: "Alimentary, My Dear Watson." (My favorite was a Jewish-Indian eatery called "Kashmir Tochus.")

Susie is not Oliver's love interest. That role now falls to the redoubtable Detective Sergeant Effie Strongitharm, although Ollie does admit to having been in love with Susie for a week just after they met at university. The way Susie will describe it, in the next Swithin mystery, is that Oliver said he wanted to make love to her very badly. She demurred because she thought he probably would.

Oliver would surely like to prepare this curried vegetable dish. It's enormously adaptable to whatever produce is lying around, remarkably colorful (if you keep the turmeric to a bare minimum), keeps and freezes well, and can be served as a main course or an accompaniment to something spicy. It also gives you a knife-wielding workout—reducing vegetables of varying shapes to the same-sized diced morsels will certainly distract you from thinking about that body in the basement for a while.

2 tablespoons olive oil	Salt and pepper, to taste
1 large onion, chopped coarsely	2 large carrots, chopped in $\frac{1}{4}$-inch dice
3 cloves garlic, crushed	2 medium zucchini, chopped in $\frac{1}{4}$-inch dice
4 teaspoon cumin seed	1 yellow squash, chopped in $\frac{1}{4}$-inch dice
2 teaspoon coriander seed	1 green, red, or yellow pepper,
1 teaspoon fenugreek	chopped in $\frac{1}{4}$-inch dice
1 teaspoon powdered ginger	1 medium turnip, chopped in $\frac{1}{4}$-inch dice
Pinch of turmeric	10 grape or cherry tomatoes,
2 cinnamon sticks	or 5 plum tomatoes, quartered
1 pint chicken or vegetable stock	1 cup golden raisins
Sprinkling of cayenne	Finely chopped parsley or cilantro

Heat a large pot or Dutch oven, big enough for all the ingredients, on top of the range. When very hot, reduce heat to medium, and add the olive oil. When the oil is hot enough, add the onions first, then the crushed garlic. Cook gently for 10 minutes, or until the onion is transparent, being careful not to scorch the garlic.

Meanwhile, toast the cumin and coriander seeds in a thick-bottomed skillet (cast iron is best) for a few minutes, until they become aromatic. Remove from heat, and place in a mortar or a coffee grinder with the fenugreek. Grind to a find powder. Sniff well.

Turn up the heat under the pot, add the ground spices, ginger, turmeric, and cinnamon sticks, and cook, stirring, for one minute. Add the stock, season with salt, pepper, and cayenne according to your tolerance, and boil for 5 minutes. (You may not need to add salt if your stock has a high sodium content.)

Add the diced carrots, zucchini, yellow squash, turnip, and pepper. Stir well, reduce heat, cover, and simmer for 10 minutes. Stir occasionally.

Add the tomatoes and raisins, and simmer, covered, for a further 10 minutes. Stir occasionally.

Just before your guests arrive, sauté some onion and bacon pieces in olive oil. This has nothing to do with the recipe, but it guarantees they'll walk in saying, "Something smells good!" Then serve the curried vegetables over plain couscous, with a sprinkling of parsley or cilantro.

Serves 4.

Some variations: For the first round of vegetables, you can substitute or add fennel, celery, potatoes, different-colored peppers, etc.

For the second round (when you add the tomatoes), you can include anything that just needs to be cooked briefly or heated, such as frozen peas, apples, mangoes, prunes (seedless and quartered) or sautéed mushrooms.

Oliver Swithin, whose children's books feature the notorious "Finsbury the Ferret," has found himself solving murders in two novels: the non-award-winning *An Embarrassment of Corpses* and *Murdering Ministers* by Alan Beechey.

Potato Curry

MAT COWARD

When I first started cooking with intent—in my late teens, in the late 1970s—I had two problems: I lived in what we British call a "bedsit," which meant I had access to a stovetop, but no oven, and I had recently become a vegetarian. Most of the vegetarian recipes I could find were either worthy and bland, or else elaborate beyond my means. This simple, filling, tasty—and above all, one-pot—dish was an exception, and became a staple of my limited repertoire. It had one other great advantage, for a young, sociable bachelor: I could prepare it early on, then re-heat it on returning from an evening in the pub, usually accompanied by a few hungry friends who lacked my culinary skills. I still cook it today, but now it's even better because the spuds and peas come from my own garden.

My series detective, DI Don Packham, is a curry aficionado, and my first novel was set on an allotment gardening site.

> 6 medium red potatoes
> 1 tablespoon vegetable oil
> ½ teaspoon cayenne pepper
> 1 teaspoon coriander
> 1 teaspoon English mustard powder
> 1 teaspoon turmeric
> 1 teaspoon cumin seeds
> 1 ½ cups of cold water
> 4 ounces shelled green peas, fresh or frozen

Evenly dice the peeled potatoes. Heat the oil in a heavy-bottomed pan, and add all spices. Cook briefly, until the spices begin to release their aroma. Add the potatoes, and stir around to evenly coat with the spices and oil. Cook on a moderate heat for 10 minutes, stirring occasionally to prevent sticking. Add the water, and simmer for about half an hour, stirring occasionally, until spuds are tender. Add the peas; cook for a few minutes more until the peas are tender.

Serve hot—or, even better, reheated the next day—with Indian bread.

Mat Coward's Packham and Mitchell series includes *Up and Down* and *In and Out*. You can visit him at http://hometown.aol.co.uk/matcoward/myhomepage/newsletter.html.

Justinian's Minimalist Egg Curry
MARY REED AND ERIC MAYER

John the Eunuch, Lord Chamberlain to Emperor Justinian, favors simple dishes. So do we. Jamborees at Constantinople's Great Palace featured banquets offering elaborate dishes like fish soufflés, wine-basted pork, honey cakes, and small game birds such as larks and thrushes served with various sauces. By contrast, plain old egg curry often appeared on dinner menus at the grammar (high) school Mary attended. This curry was extremely popular, perhaps due to the lingering influence of the great days of the British Raj or possibly general relief that the meal that day did not feature the ubiquitous boiled cabbage, one of those smells inevitably intertwined with memories of schooldays.

We've dubbed our version minimalist because the original recipe (obtained from a friend over a decade ago) called for additional ingredients, but over the years we've gradually pared it down to the essentials. It's a hearty dish that John would certainly enjoy. Unfortunately for him, however, although he's rich enough to buy any amount of spices and his elderly servant Peter would be overjoyed at the opportunity to cook a more elaborate dish than usual for his employer, in the sixth century the all important tomato was still lurking about undiscovered in the New World. Even so, since Justinian was vegetarian he'd doubtless approve of our recipe.

> 2 medium onions
> 15-ounce can tomato sauce
> 15 ounces milk
> 2 tart apples (Granny Smiths are best)
> Curry powder to taste
> 2 to 4 hard-boiled eggs

Slice and fry the onions, and set aside. Mix the tomato sauce and milk in another pan. Peel and dice the apples, and add them to the tomato sauce and milk mixture. Add curry powder to taste to the tomato sauce, milk, and apple mixture (we add 4 tablespoons), and simmer until the apples begin to soften. Add the cooked onions to the mixture, and simmer for a few moments. Slice the hard-boiled eggs, add to the mixture, and simmer until the eggs are heated through. Serve with rice, and a garnish of pineapple and sliced bananas.

Mary Reed and Eric Mayer are co-authors of the John the Eunuch mystery series. Titles published thus far are *One For Sorrow, Two For Joy, Three For A Letter,* and *Four For a Boy.*

Killer Veggie Medley

M. K. PRESTON

*C*hantalene Morrell is a vegetarian, but she loves to eat. Since she grows her own vegetables, the ingredients for this medley come fresh from her garden. It's a quick and healthy dish that can be served as an entree with garlic bread, as a side dish, or over angel hair pasta that's been tossed with a sprinkle of olive oil.

> 2 tablespoons olive oil
> 1 zucchini squash, cut in ¼-inch thick semi-circles
> 1 small yellow squash, cut same as zucchini
> 6 baby carrots, halved lengthwise
> Half a purple onion, cut in chunks
> 1 red pepper, cut in ⅛-inch rings
> Seasoned salt and lemon pepper to taste
> 1 tablespoon red wine vinegar

Heat the olive oil in a large skillet or wok, and add all the vegetables at once. Sprinkle with seasoned salt and lemon pepper, and stir fry over medium heat 5 to 10 minutes, until the vegetables are tender-crisp. Just before removing from heat, sprinkle on the red wine vinegar and mix lightly. Eat while it's hot.

M. K. Preston is the author of *Perhaps She'll Die* and *Song of the Bones,* which feature Chantalene Morrell, the Oklahoma-born daughter of a Gypsy mother and a red-neck father.

ACCOMPLICES

Mma Ramotswe's Boiled Pumpkin with Botswana Ostrich

ALEXANDER MCCALL SMITH

Mma Ramotswe, founder and owner of the No. 1 Ladies' Detective Agency in Botswana, believes in a traditional approach to food and does not like these modern dishes which thin people like to eat. She is a traditionally-built lady, and she believes that it is best to eat food which makes you strong. This is a dish which she likes to make for her fiancé, Mr J.L.B. Matekoni, proprietor of Tlokweng Road Speedy Motors and undoubtedly the finest mechanic in Botswana.

Take one pumpkin. Make sure that the pumpkin is round and has a good yellow color. Chop the pumpkin into pieces, using a large knife. Take out the flesh of the pumpkin. Then remove the seeds of the pumpkin and put them in a dish. They can be dried and then planted back in the earth to grow more pumpkins.

Put the chunks of pumpkin into boiling water and let them boil away until the pumpkin is soft. Make sure that there is salt in the water. Take the pumpkin out of the water and put many lumps of butter in it and mash it all up. Add more salt if you need to, and some pepper, which may be sprinkled on top of the pumpkin. That is the pumpkin. It is finished now.

In the meantime, you must take some ostrich steaks. The best ostriches in the world live in Botswana. They are strong birds and their meat is rich. Even in America you can buy this meat, if you are lucky. Put the meat in a frying pan and grill it nice and quickly. Then take it out and serve it on the plate with the pumpkin and also, if you wish, with a green vegetable that you have cooked separately.

This is a very delicious meal. Afterwards, you may eat some cake and drink a cup of red bush tea. Red bush tea is best flavored with some honey. It is very refreshing.

Alexander McCall Smith's No. 1 Ladies' Detective Agency books include *The No. 1 Ladies' Detective Agency, Tears of the Giraffe, Morality for Beautiful Girls,* and *The Kalahari Typing School for Men.*

Southwestern Black Bean Salad

LORA ROBERTS

$\mathcal{M}$ost of my mysteries take place in California, home of fictional sleuths Liz Sullivan and Bridget Montrose (Bridget was the viewpoint character in my recent *Another Fine Mess*). Salads are popular in that state known for its produce. This black bean and corn salad tastes best if you cook your own black beans and find the freshest corn on the cob at the farmer's market. But you can always fall back on the more convenient canned beans and frozen corn. Such a salad would be unknown to the characters in my next book, *The Affair of the Incognito Tenant*, which takes place 100 years ago in England and features, among other characters, Sherlock Holmes.

2 cups cooked black beans (if canned, rinse well)
2 cups cooked corn kernels, cut off the cob or defrosted
½ cup diced red bell pepper
½ cup diced red onion
¼ cup minced cilantro
¼ cup minced parsley
½ cup vinaigrette dressing (recipe follows)

Combine the beans, corn, bell pepper, onion, cilantro, and parsley in a bowl. Add the dressing, mix well. Refrigerate until serving, or overnight.

Vinaigrette

1 clove garlic, crushed
½ teaspoon sugar
½ teaspoon salt
1 teaspoon cumin
¼ teaspoon cayenne pepper
2 teaspoon prepared mustard
⅓ cup olive oil
¼ cup balsamic vinegar

Combine the garlic, sugar, salt, spices, and mustard in a small lidded jar. Mix well, crushing the ingredients into a paste. Add the olive oil and vinegar, put on the lid, and shake well.

Lora Roberts is the author of the Bridget Montrose Mysteries, which include *Revolting Development* and *Another Fine Mess*. She is also the author of several novels featuring Liz Sullivan, including *Murder in a Nice Neighborhood* and *Murder Bone by Bone*.

Jennifer's 'Twas a Dark and Stormy Broccoli Salad

JUDY FITZWATER

When Jennifer Marsh isn't chained to her computer writing a mystery novel she hopes will finally sell, she works part-time in her friend Dee Dee's catering service. Jennifer's special expertise is flowers she makes from vegetables and forms into wreaths and bouquets. She also does most of Dee Dee's vegetable dishes and salads. (Jennifer is a vegetarian and, in *Dying for a Clue*, makes chicken and dumplings, without the chicken, for a church supper.) This recipe is one of her favorites and one of mine as well. It's easy to make and absolutely delicious.

> 2 large bunches of fresh broccoli (florets only)
> ⅔ cup imitation bacon bits
> ½ cup diced onion
> ⅔ cup raisins
> ⅔ cup chopped peanuts

Dressing

> 2 cups mayonnaise
> ¼ cup sugar
> 6 teaspoons vinegar

Mix the dressing ingredients together and toss with the salad ingredients. Serve the same day.

Judy Fitzwater writes the Jennifer Marsh Mysteries, which debuted with the Agatha-nominated *Dying to Get Published* and has continued through six books, including *Dying to be Murdered* and *Dying to Get Her Man*.

Mamie Barnard's Tomato Salad
LINDA BERRY

I think my grandmother invented this recipe during the depression. Doesn't it sound like something a poor farm wife might invent to feed her family? My Aunt Mildred says she doesn't think anybody outside the family has ever had it. (I say it tastes better than you'd expect.) It's comfort food for my mother's family. In *Death and the Icebox*, I assign the recipe to Trudy Roundtree's family and she makes it for her cousin, Henry Huckabee—her boss, who happens to be the Chief of Police in Ogeechee, Georgia.

> Canned tomatoes
> Saltines
> Hard-boiled eggs
> Sweet pickles
> Salt
> Pepper
> Sugar
> Mayonnaise

Do not drain the juice from the tomatoes. Crumble enough saltine crackers into the tomatoes to absorb the juice. Add chopped hard-boiled eggs, cubed pickles, salt, pepper, a pinch of sugar, and enough mayonnaise (*not* Miracle Whip!) to hold it together.

Linda Berry describes her Trudy Roundtree mysteries—*Death and the Easter Bunny, Death and the Hubcap*, and *Death and the Icebox*—as "soft-boiled and mixed with grit."

Victoria Trumbull's Boston Baked Beans

CYNTHIA RIGGS

Victoria Trumbull, 92-year-old poet, was born and raised on Martha's Vineyard. After she backed her car into the Meals on Wheels van, police chief Mary Kathleen O'Neill, a newcomer to the Island, confiscated Victoria's driver's license, but promised to take the old lady wherever she needed to go. As a result, the chief is now stuck with an ancient sidekick. A sidekick who is related to half the Island and knows where all the skeletons are buried.

Every Saturday night, for as long as she can remember, Victoria has dined on a traditional Boston baked bean supper. Now she entertains with her bean suppers, laying her fine china, her silver, and her crystal stemware on her freshly ironed damask tablecloth. She's found that an invitation to her bean supper is an excellent way to trap an unsuspecting murderer.

She cooks her Boston baked beans in the traditional way, soaking dried yellow eyed beans (or navy beans) overnight, then cooking them all day on Saturday in the same bean pot her own grandmother used. Here's her recipe.

> 1 pound dried yellow eyed beans (or navy beans)
> Water
> 1 medium onion
> ¼ pound salt pork
> ⅓ cup brown sugar
> ⅓ cup dark molasses
> 1 teaspoon dried mustard
> 1 teaspoon salt

On Friday night, put the dried beans in a large (4-quart) container or Dutch oven. Cover them with about 3 quarts of water, and let them soak overnight. On Saturday morning, cook the beans on top of the stove for about 1 to 1 ½ hours using the same water. Test for doneness by blowing on one or two beans. If the thin skin cracks and curls, the beans are done. Drain the beans, saving the water they were cooked in for the next step. The beans will be a pale color.

Score the top of the onion, cutting it about halfway through, and put it in the bottom of a crockery bean pot (a heavy covered casserole dish will do, but it's not traditional). Spoon the beans on top of the onion.

Score the rind of the salt pork, turn it over and score the soft part. Bury the salt pork in the beans, rind side down, leaving the white part exposed.

In a bowl mix the brown sugar, molasses, mustard, and salt with about a cup of the bean water. Pour the mixture over the beans. Add more bean water until the beans are covered.

Cover the bean pot and set it on a pan (to catch any drips) in the middle of the oven. Cook in a slow oven, 325 degrees, until ready to serve, 4 to 6 hours. Check the beans every hour or so to make sure they are still covered with liquid. Add water as needed. Be sure to keep the beans moist. As time passes, the beans will get darker and darker until they are a rich mahogany color.

Victoria serves her Boston baked beans with warmed brown bread (she used to make her own, but now she uses canned), hot dogs, and a green salad. Her neighbor down the road prefers coleslaw to salad.

The only fragrance to compare with that of baking beans is the smell of baking bread. A perfume to throw the most heinous character off guard.

Cynthia Riggs is the author of three mysteries set on Martha's Vineyard and featuring 92-year-old poet Victoria Trumbull: *Deadly Nightshade, The Cranefly Orchid Murders*, and *The Cemetery Yew*.

Dorothy's Dreadful Dinner
LILLIAN STEWART CARL

A running joke in *Ashes to Ashes* is the 50s-style cuisine served up by Dorothy, the housekeeper. Rebecca and Michael, the protagonists, refuse to eat it. Little do they realize just what a wise decision they're making, when Dorothy's food becomes part of the antagonist's plot.

> *Rebecca…peered into the basket. A congealed salad peered back at her, queasy orange Jell-O clotted with carrot strips and canned pineapple. Another dish held gray hunks of hamburger meat laced with green peas and instant rice like bits of styrofoam. Exhaling through pursed lips, Rebecca closed the basket….*

The Salad

1 small package orange Jell-O
½ to 1 cup grated carrots (use a very large and very old carrot, preferably one with whiskers)
1 small can crushed pineapple, undrained

Cook the Jell-O according to the package directions. Stir in the grated carrot and the crushed pineapple. Pour it all into a medium-size mold. Refrigerate. Unmold. If you've followed the directions and haven't squashed the liquid out of the pineapple, you'll have a fluorescent oozing mound.

The Casserole

1 pound ground beef, the cheapest you can find
1 cup frozen peas, preferably freezer-burned
2 cups instant rice, undercooked so it's still crunchy
1 14 ½-ounce can stewed tomatoes
2 ounces American cheese, the kind that comes in canary-yellow blocks
Salt and pepper

Brown the ground beef, stirring it around until it's cooked to the consistency of rubber. Don't bother pouring off the grease. Dump the meat, the (still-frozen) peas, the rice, and the stewed tomatoes into a casserole dish and mix. Add a dash of salt, and, if you're feeling extravagant, pepper. Grate the cheese over the top. Bake in a 350 degree oven for about an hour, or until the edges are dried and crusty. To complete the meal, serve with grocery-store white bread, the kind that can double as a sponge.

Ashes to Ashes in the first in Lillian Stewart Carl's mystery series that also includes *Dust to Dust* and *Garden of Thorn*. Visit her at www.lillianstewartcarl.com.

Pearl Zak's Pudding
G. H. EPHRON

There were many good reasons (including comic relief) for us to create a feisty, independent Jewish mother for mystery sleuth-cum-forensic psychologist Dr. Peter Zak. She gives us an excuse to write about food. Here's the recipe for the noodle pudding Pearl serves Peter and investigator Annie Squires in *Obsessed*—it's "dense and chewy with a crisp outer layer, savory—not sweet the way some people make it." It's the combination of salt and sugar that makes it work.

Preheat the oven to 350 degrees. Butter the baking dish.

> 16 ounces flat egg noodles
> 2 cups (16-ounce container) cottage cheese
> 1 cup (8-ounce container) of sour cream
> ½ cup milk
> 2 tablespoons granulated sugar
> 1 tablespoon salt
> 2 tablespoons butter, cut into small pieces

Boil the noodles according to package directions; drain and return to pan. Add the remaining ingredients. Pour the noodle mixture into a large shallow buttered baking dish (for lots of crispy edges; use a smaller deeper buttered dish). Bake at 350 degrees until the edges are browned—about 1 hour.

The Dr. Peter Zak mystery series—*Delusion*, *Addiction*, *Amnesia*, and *Obsessed*—features a Boston-based forensic psychologist. The author, G. H. Ephron, is really two people: writer Hallie Ephron and neuropsychologist Donald Davidoff, Ph.D.

Marla's Noodle Kugel
NANCY J. COHEN

Marla Shore, hairstylist sleuth in the Bad Hair Day Mysteries, shares my Jewish roots. One way to portray her ethnic heritage is through food. Marla contributes this dish as a volunteer for the Child Drowning Prevention Coalition when she attends a community fair in *Murder by Manicure*. It makes a good accompaniment for roast meats.

16-ounce bag wide egg noodles
4 eggs, beaten
½ cup sugar
½ pound margarine, melted
¼ teaspoon cinnamon
1 20-ounce can crushed pineapple, drained
Juice from a fresh lemon
1 or 2 tablespoons cinnamon sugar
1 cup cornflake crumbs

Preheat the oven to 350 degrees. Cook the noodles in boiling water for 8 minutes, then drain and rinse under cold water. Stir a few noodles into the beaten eggs. Pour the eggs into a bowl with the noodles, and mix. Add the sugar, melted margarine, cinnamon, pineapple, and lemon juice. Stir until blended.

Put into a greased 11-by-14-inch baking pan. Sprinkle the cornflake crumbs and cinnamon sugar on top. Bake for approximately 50 minutes, or until browned and bubbly.

Options: Cut the margarine to ¼ pound and add 2 cups sour cream, *or* add 1 teaspoon vanilla instead of lemon juice *or* add ½ cup raisins.

Nancy J. Cohen is author of the Bad Hair Day Mysteries: *Murder by Manicure*, *Body Wave*, and *Highlights to Heaven*. Learn more at http://nancyjcohen.com.

TOUGH COOKIES

All Time Greatest Chocolate Chip Cookies

CLAUDIA BISHOP

I write a series of mysteries featuring amateur detectives Meg, a gourmet chef, and Quill, the manager of a twenty-seven room inn. I'm a binge writer. Just like a binge eater, I starve myself of writing until the very last minute, when I can't stand it anymore and then I write like mad seven days a week, until the darn novel is finished. I write for four hours, stop, eat, nap, and then start the cycle all over again. I like working this way. (I didn't say I was a *smart* mystery writer.) And I like it even more because this marathon run is the only time I allow myself these cookies. These are—honest to God—the best chocolate chip cookies in the world.

> 1 cup salted butter, softened to room temperature
> ¾ cup dark brown sugar, packed
> ¾ cup white sugar
> 2 extra-large eggs
> 1 to 2 tablespoons pure vanilla extract
> ¾ teaspoon baking powder
> ¾ teaspoon baking soda
> 2 ½ to 2 ¾ cups flour
> 1 pound semi-sweet chocolate chips
> 2 cups chopped walnuts
> 2 cups shredded coconut

Throw first 7 ingredients into a glass mixing bowl, and beat with an electric beater for the amount of time it takes to sing "Big Spender" from *Sweet Charity,* or until the mixture has paled and fluffed. Add 1 cup of regular white flour. Beat with the beater. Add a second cup of white flour. Beat with the beater. Add about ½ cup to ¾ cup flour and beat in with a wooden spoon. Mixture should stick to the ceiling if you throw a handful skywards. Add the semi-sweet chocolate chips; chopped walnuts, and shredded coconut. Mix with wooden spoon.

Drop very large spoonfuls onto a buttered cookie sheet. Bake in a 375 degree oven for 15 minutes or so. (Cookies should turn from the ochre of the dough to a pale toast color and be soft in the middle.)

If any readers figure out the calorie/carbohydrate/fat content of these cookies, *please* don't tell me.

Claudia Bishop is the author of the popular Hemlock Falls mystery series including *Fried By Jury* and *Boil and Bubble.* She is also the co-editor of *Death Dines at 8:30,* an anthology of sixteen stories of "crime and cuisine."

Chocolate Chip Crunch Cookies
JOANNE FLUKE

*I*n book one of the Hannah Swensen Mysteries, Hannah bakes her sister's favorite cookies, "Chocolate Chip Crunch." I baked over two thousand of these cookies for my book signing at the *Los Angeles Times* Festival of Books. The cookies were such a big hit, I came home with nothing but crumbs in the bottom of the cookie jar.

> 1 cup butter (2 sticks)
> 1 cup white sugar
> 1 cup brown sugar
> 2 teaspoons baking soda
> 1 teaspoon salt
> 2 teaspoons vanilla
> 2 beaten eggs (you can beat them up with a fork)
> 2 cups corn flakes
> 2 ½ cups flour (no need to sift)
> 1 to 2 cups chocolate chips

Preheat oven to 375 degrees, place rack in the middle position.

Melt the butter, add the sugars, and mix. Add the baking soda, salt, vanilla, and beaten eggs. Mix well. Crush the corn flakes with your hands. Add the crushed corn flakes, flour, and chocolate chips, mixing thoroughly after each addition.

Place walnut-size balls of dough on a greased cookie sheet, 12 to a standard sheet. Flatten the dough balls with a floured or greased spatula.

Bake at 375 degrees for 8 to 10 minutes. *Note*: If the cookies spread out too much on the pan, reduce oven temperature to 350 degrees and do not flatten the dough balls before baking.

Cool on cookie sheet for 2 minutes and then remove to a wire rack to complete cooling.

Yield: 5 to 6 dozen, depending on cookie size.

Joanne Fluke's cookie-baking sleuth Hannah Swensen has appeared in *Chocolate Chip Cookie Murder*, *Strawberry Shortcake Murder*, *Blueberry Muffin Murder*, *Lemon Meringue Pie Murder*, and *Fudge Cupcake Murder*. At least seven original cookie and dessert recipes are included in each book. She posts a new recipe every month at her website, www.MurderSheBaked.com.

Killer New Mexican Wedding Cookies

SARAH LOVETT

*T*he mystery of Grandma's cake: Forensic psychologist Dr. Sylvia Strange and I were wedded to our respective fiances within months of each other. At each Santa Fe ceremony, this traditional wedding cookie was served up with a red chile twist. During my nuptial celebration, the cookies filled the gap while the bakery sent a driver racing out to deliver the cake. Actually, to *exchange* cakes. Earlier in the day, a sheet wedding cake had been delivered (as requested) and refrigerated in its box. When it came time to present the cake for ritual cutting, the box was opened, and—much to everyone's surprise—the dessert in question was decorated with red sneakers and bowling balls; the message read: *Happy 80th Grandma!*

Needless to say, at another party across town, Grandma was also puzzled by her cake, which sported yellow and pink roses, a cowboy bride and groom, and an encouraging message *Michael & Sarah—Giddyup!*

The cakes were returned to their rightful parties, but in the meantime, these cookies added just the right amount of killer spice. This recipe is a group effort courtesy of Sylvia's best friend, Rosie Sanchez and her *abuelita*, and my friends, Emily Swantner, who runs Santa Fe's Epicurean Odyssey, and Marilyn Abraham.

Preheat oven to 325 degrees

> 1 cup pecans, ground fine
> 2 cups all-purpose flour
> ¼ teaspoon salt
> ¼ teaspoon *medium hot* or ½ teaspoon *mild* New Mexican red chile powder
> 1 cup softened butter
> ¼ cup sugar
> 2 teaspoons vanilla
> ¼ cup confectioner's sugar

In a large mixing bowl combine the nuts, flour, salt, and chile powder. Mix well.

In another bowl, beat the butter; add the sugar and vanilla. Add the flour mixture to the butter mixture, and mix until you get a crumbly batter. Shape into small balls, and place on an ungreased cookie sheet. Bake for 20 minutes. Remove the cookies from the sheet, and cool on racks. When cool, shake a few at a time in a bag containing confectioner's sugar.

Yields: 2 to 3 dozen

In Sarah Lovett's psychological who-done-its—*Dark Alchemy, Dangerous Attachments,* and *Dantes' Inferno*—forensic psychologist Dr. Sylvia Strange (who has been described as Nancy Drew on steroids) outwits some of the most twisted minds in the American criminal justice system.

Beacon Hill Cookies

DONNA ANDREWS

*L*ike most of my family's favorite recipes, we didn't make this one up. Someone found it somewhere—in the *Newport News Daily Press*? In an old cookbook? On the back of a package of chocolate chips? We'll never know. In this case, the someone was my mother's mother, whose maiden name, Langslow, I appropriated for the heroine of my first book, *Murder with Peacocks*.

Whenever we set off on a family vacation, Mummaw would make a batch of these cookies and pack them in a metal cookie tin painted to look like blue and white Wedgewood china. I have many fond memories of eating them, along with fried chicken, while strolling through old graveyards—that was usually where my family picnicked on vacation. Sometimes my genealogist Dad wanted to search them for ancestors; sometimes my history buff mother wanted to hunt down people she'd read about; and sometimes we just enjoyed the landscaping. And besides, it's free.

Maybe it's not surprising that I became a mystery writer.

> 1 cup (6 ounces) semi-sweet chocolate chips
> 2 egg whites
> ½ cup sugar
> ½ teaspoon vanilla
> ½ teaspoon vinegar
> ¾ cup chopped walnuts (optional)
> Dash of salt

Melt the chocolate over hot water. Beat the egg whites with a dash of salt until foamy. Gradually add the sugar, beating well. Beat the sugar and egg whites until stiff peaks form. Beat in the vanilla and vinegar. Fold in the chocolate and walnuts.

Drop by teaspoonfuls on greased cookie sheet. Bake in moderate oven (350 degrees) for 10 minutes.

Note: Don't let the batter sit, or the beaten egg whites will start falling. The faster you get it onto the sheet and into the oven, the better the finished cookies will be.

Makes approximately 3 dozen cookies.

Ornamental blacksmith Meg Langslow's first appearance in *Murder with Peacocks* won Donna Andrews the Agatha, Anthony, Barry, and Romantic Times awards for Best First Mystery, as well as the Lefty Award for the funniest mystery of that year. Other titles include *Murder with Puffins* and *Crouching Buzzard, Leaping Loon*. Learn more about Meg Langslow and Donna's new sci-fi/mystery character, Turing Hopper, at her website: http://donnaandrews.com.

Murder On The Menu
JANET A. RUDOLPH

Culinary Crime is one of the most appetizing and sensual themes in mystery fiction. There are so many tantalizing and succulent ways to dispose of someone gastronomically, so it is not surprising that I devoted four issues of the *Mystery Readers Journal* to Culinary Crime, taught five courses complete with food tastings from the books, sans that "special" murderous ingredient, moderated many panels on culinary crime, and produced and choreographed Nero Wolfe, Lord Peter Wimsey and Sherlock Holmes dinners as well as numerous Agatha Christie/Dorothy L. Sayers high teas. When it came time to name my interactive mystery company, what else could I have chosen but Murder on the Menu? What surprises me is the number of calls I receive from people who think Murder on the Menu is a catering company. We only cater to their entertainment desires. Would you hire a caterer named Murder on the Menu? Well, you might if you had an ironic and sinister scenario for a dinner guest. It's a concept worthy of Lucretia Borgia, but what would be your chances for repeat business?

The most memorable culinary interactive mystery play I've ever written had a French theme about Marie Antoinette's *Gateau au Chocolat* with blood oranges. Yes, when Marie Antoinette said "Let Them Eat Cake" she was referring to this specific recipe. As the play unfolds, the recipe is found, authenticated, and stolen again. This particular Murder on the Menu event was hosted by members of a French epicurean club, *et bien sur*, the dessert was *fantastique*. I've also been able to kill with food for events for the National Association of Catering Executives. However, since most people are dining and interacting during a Murder on the Menu production, I usually shy away from using what they're eating as a method of malice.

Of the ten Culinary Crime panels I've moderated over the years, one of my favorites was the one at the Monterey Bouchercon in 1997. I envisioned cooking demonstrations with each author cooking up something from his/her novel, but alas, the facility wasn't open to that. As an alternative, I assigned each panelist a different course. Not only did they need to come up with a delectable recipe for that course, but they needed to include a culinary means of demise. I printed up all the recipes and distributed the menu to all attendees, omitting the murderous ingredient or technique, of course. We are a devious and mischievous lot, we mystery readers and writers, but we never lack for divine sustenance.

And we're all Dying for Chocolate. Here's a Killer Brownie Recipe.

Killer Brownies

1 pound unsalted butter
1 pound plus 12 ounces semisweet chocolate chips
6 ounces unsweetened chocolate
6 extra-large eggs
3 tablespoons instant coffee granules
2 tablespoons pure vanilla extract
1 ½ cups sugar
1 ¼ cups all-purpose flour
1 tablespoon baking powder
1 teaspoon salt
3 cups chopped walnuts (optional)

Preheat oven to 350 degrees. Butter and flour a 12-by-18-by-1-inch baking pan.

Melt together the butter, 1 pound of chocolate chips, and the unsweetened chocolate in a medium bowl over simmering water. Allow to cool slightly. In a large bowl, stir (do not beat) together the eggs, vanilla, coffee granules, and sugar. Stir warm chocolate mixture and allow to cool to room temperature.

Mix together 1 cup of the flour, baking powder, and salt. Add to the cooled chocolate mixture. Toss the walnuts and 12 ounces of chocolate chips in a medium bowl with ¼ cup of flour, then add to the chocolate batter. Pour into the baking pan.

Bake for 20 minutes; then rap the baking sheet against the oven's shelf to force air to escape between the pan and brownie dough. Bake for 15 minutes more, until a toothpick comes out clean. Do not over bake. Allow to cool. Refrigerate and cut into squares.

Of course I never wait and the brownies sometimes crumble, but who cares? They're great hot from the oven. Just be careful not to drop crumbs on the mystery you're reading.

Janet A. Rudolph is editor of the *Mystery Readers Journal*, director of Mystery Readers International, and a teacher of mystery fiction. A long-time contributor to the mystery genre, she received her Ph.D. in religious mystery fiction. She writes customized mystery scripts, a challenging twist on the mystery genre, for her company, Murder on the Menu, California's #1 interactive mystery event company. Her websites are www.murderonthemenu.com and www.mysteryreaders.org.

Bulletproof Peanut Butter Balls
DEBORAH DONNELLY

*C*arnegie Kincaid, wedding planner and sleuth, organizes some elaborately catered banquets. But in her own kitchen, the watchword is "Keep it simple, sweetheart." Her favorite recipe couldn't be simpler, or more addictive!

½ cup (1 stick) butter (or margarine, but butter makes firmer cookies)
20 ounces (2 cups) peanut butter (I use Jif)
1 pound powdered sugar
3 cups Rice Krispies
12 ounces semi-sweet chocolate chips

On low heat, melt the peanut butter and butter. In a large bowl, stir together the powdered sugar and Rice Krispies. Pour the melted mixture over the dry ingredients, mix, and roll into ½-inch balls. Chill the balls on cookie sheets until firm.

Melt the chocolate chips in small batches, on the stove or in the microwave. Dip the balls in chocolate, return to the cookie sheets, and chill.

Once cold, these can be packed into tins and frozen. They probably keep for weeks, but they never last that long!

Makes about 4 ½ dozen.

Deborah Donnelly's paperback series, the Wedding Planner Mysteries, includes *Veiled Threats*, *Died to Match*, and *May the Best Man Die*. Visit www.deborahdonnelly.org for a sneak preview.

Disappearing Chocolate Cookies

(Chocolate Crinkle Cookies)

KATHERINE AYRES

These are a family favorite and they disappear faster than a cat burglar at dawn. They even disappear before baking if children help in the preparations which does raise the possibility of food poisoning—all those raw eggs! But the thief is easily identified by a skilled detective—chocolate stuck to the palm of the hand, smudged on the chin, smeared on the shirt, and the tell-tale trace of powdered sugar along the upper lip. You'll note that premeditation is required in this endeavor, as the dough must sit overnight in the fridge before baking. Enjoy!

½ cup corn oil
4 squares melted unsweetened chocolate
2 cups sugar
4 eggs
2 teaspoons vanilla
½ teaspoon salt
2 cups flour
2 teaspoons baking powder
1 cup powdered sugar

Mix the corn oil, melted chocolate, and sugar, and blend in 1 egg at a time. Add the vanilla. Stir in the salt, flour, and baking powder. Refrigerate overnight.

Drop 1 teaspoon of dough at a time into powdered sugar, and roll into a ball. Place on a greased cookie sheet. Bake 10 to 12 minutes at 350 degrees.

These cookies are so good, I usually double the recipe and freeze some.

Katherine Ayres writes mysteries for kids. Recent titles include *Voices at Whisper Bend*, *Under Copp's Hill* and *Macaroni Boy*, which although it sounds like a foodie mystery might actually cause you to lose your appetite. Learn more at www.chatham.edu/users/faculty/kayres.

Sticks and Stones
ROBERT WEIBEZAHL

$\mathcal{M}$y daughter Katie was just four years old when *A Taste of Murder* was published, but she accompanied me to many of the bookstore events celebrating the book. At those events, I usually served Death by Chocolate Cake, from the recipe that my partner in culinary crime, Jo Grossman, provided from the menu of her erstwhile Mystery Café. That cake "from Daddy's cookbook" became a familiar item around our house on birthdays and such.

Just around the time we started working on this second volume, Katie figured out that the cake recipe was not "mine"—a crushing blow to her now-almost-eight-year-old sensibility. "Which recipe is yours?" she wanted to know.

"Well, none really," I said, sensing her mounting disappointment.

"Will you have a recipe in the new book?" she asked.

"I guess I could," I said.

Then I thought: Why not provide the very recipe that Katie herself invented when she was just seven (precocious thing!)—a clever, easy-to-make snack concoction that she dubbed "Sticks and Stones." Of course, Katie could argue that I still don't have a recipe in the book—*she* does. But somehow I don't think she'll care.

> 1 cup mini marshmallows
> 1 cup chocolate chips
> 1 cup nuts
> 1 handful thin pretzel sticks
> Some Pepperidge Farm goldfish

Mix the marshmallows and chocolate chips together in a microwave-safe bowl, and melt them in the microwave, 1 to 2 minutes. Stir the mixture a bit, but don't blend completely. In another bowl, mix together the nuts, pretzels, and goldfish. Combine the chocolate/marshmallow mixture with the dry ingredients. Spread the whole mess on wax paper to cool at room temperature. Once cool, break up into chunks and eat!

The co-author of *A Taste of Murder* and *A Second Helping of Murder*, Robert Weibezahl made his mystery fiction debut with the story "Judge and Jury," published in *Futures Mysterious Anthology Magazine*.

The Agony of the Leaves
MEG CHITTENDEN

Meg Chittenden delivered a version of this essay at a tea party during Bouchercon in Milwaukee in 1999. That was also the Bouchercon at which A Taste of Murder *was launched, so we have a special fondness for the event, for Meg, and of course, for tea.*

Tea was first discovered by the Chinese emperor Shen Nung in 2737 B.C. Of course he didn't know it was 2737 B.C., he had a different way of looking at things. But he did know a good thing when he found it.

The tea plant (*Thea sinensis, Camellia thea*, or *Camellia sinensis*) is an evergreen related to the camellia and native to India, China and Japan. It requires a warm climate with plenty of rain. In its natural state, it grows to about 30 feet, but for commercial use is pruned to bush size.

Leaves are picked at just the right moment. For black teas (some of the most popular are English breakfast, Darjeeling, and Orange Pekoe), the leaves are crushed and exposed to air, then rolled and crushed and again exposed to air, this time to ferment, before they are fired (heated); oolong teas are partially fermented, green tea isn't fermented at all. Nor is white tea, which is the most minimally processed of all. A cup of black tea has about ⅓ the amount of caffeine present in a cup of coffee; green and white teas contain even less.

In China, tea was produced on a commercial scale by the eighth century. It was introduced to Europe in the 17th century by the Dutch East India Company, and its popularity helped spur the opening of East Asia to Western commerce. In colonial America, a tax on tea led to the Boston Tea Party of 1773.

How to Brew a Perfect Cup of Tea

Fill your kettle with cold pure water. (I distill all my drinking water and I like an electric kettle.) If you are making black tea, bring the water to a rolling boil, then immediately pour it onto the tea leaves or teabags in the pot. When the boiling water hits the loose tea, the leaves unfurl and release their flavor; this is called "the Agony of the Leaves." I had never heard of the agony of the leaves until recently. I'm not sure now that I can ever use loose tea again. Maybe tea leaves are like plants and can actually feel pain.

If making green or oolong or white tea, the water should be off the boil. (I don't know if this makes it less agonizing, but it makes for good tea.)

You should always make your tea in a pot. Unless you are Russian, in which case, you may use a samovar. My grandmother favored a brown pot, which she insisted was better than a white pot. I use a blue willow pot and haven't noticed any difference, but I like to make green tea in a black iron teapot—I have a Chinese one with a wonderfully fierce-looking dragon etched on it.

When making black tea, preheat your teapot by filling it with hot water then emptying it. (Most American restaurants have never heard of this procedure, and when it is suggested to them they react with great alarm.)

If you are using loose tea, measure the tea. I use 1 teaspoon to a cup with an extra spoonful for the pot. You may use a tea ball, if you really wish. I don't believe in it myself, I think it gives the tea a metallic taste. I do however use teabags quite often. They are less messy, though perhaps not quite as good for taste.

You must let the tea steep. Where I come from, which is the north east coast of England, aka Geordie country, once coal mining country, we say we mash the tea. I've no idea why.

Next, and most important for black tea, you must cover the pot with a cozy to keep the tea warm. This also makes a huge difference to the strength and taste of the tea. If you use teabags you can remove them before pouring the tea, this prevents the remainder from getting too strong.

Tea in England is most usually taken with milk and sugar. My mother always insisted on pouring the milk into the cup before pouring the tea—it made a big difference in the taste, she said. I gave up sugar and now drink my tea black. Drink it any way you like it, with lemon if you prefer. Or iced. (Something I've never brought myself to do.) My grandmother used to put the teapot on the hob—a sort of grate sticking out from the front of the coal fire. She'd let it sit there and the tea (and the teapot) would get blacker and blacker. She liked it, she used to say, when you could stand the spoon up in it.

I drink quite a lot of green tea. This horrified my father when I confessed to it. But a study by the National Cancer Institute indicates that green tea and white tea may protect against certain types of cancer. Both have a high vitamin content. Besides which, I like them.

The Japanese have an amazing tea ceremony. If you ever get the chance to see it, do so. I have a friend in Tokyo who spent years learning how to do the tea ceremony properly.

English people have great faith in the healing power of tea. Ever since Anna, the 7th Duchess of Bedford (1788-1861), conceived the idea of afternoon tea to stem hunger pangs between lunch and dinner, the English have served it with delectable foods. My mother would bake a dozen scones, slice them, wrap a silver sixpenny piece in grease-proof paper and place it inside one scone. Whoever was lucky enough to get that scone was allowed to keep the sixpence, and occasionally broke a tooth.

Finger sandwiches are traditional accompaniments, as are teacakes—light, flat, sweet, and rather large buns with raisins or sultanas in them—which are sliced and toasted and buttered. Crumpets are toasted and buttered too. Scones are sometimes served with Devon cream and strawberry preserves, which is not a bad way to have them. I used to like them with lemon curd on them. Or Lyle's golden syrup.

A lot of my memories of childhood are tied to tea. I heard once that tea made a good setting lotion for the hair. I had hair that refused to curl, so I tried it. And of course made my tea the way I always did, with sugar in it. Do not try this at home.

One of my aunts was famous for always saying to guests when she was ready for them to leave. "Would you like a cup of tea before you go?" If we were sick, or sad, or unnaturally happy, we were given tea. If we got sunburned, cloths were dipped in tea and applied to the sore places. Worked very well too. We always had tea when we got up in the morning, and tea with breakfast, and a cup before leaving the house, tea with lunch, afternoon tea, tea with dinner or supper, a nice cup of tea before bed.

When visitors came, we never had to worry about what to serve them—tea, of course. If someone died everyone had a cup of tea. If someone got married, everyone had tea—well, maybe some Mumm's champagne too. Tea is always served in fine cups, not mugs, and the cups should have saucers beneath them. You should not pour the tea into the saucer to cool it—though I've known people who did. You should never crook your little finger while drinking tea—only people who wish to appear refined, but have no hope of doing so, adopt this mannerism.

One of the favorite old nursery rhymes in England is "Polly put the kettle on, we'll all have tea." By rights (in my opinion) it should be the national anthem.

I'll leave you with this quote, from Sydney Smith, writing in Lady Holland's Memoir—"Thank God for Tea! What would the world do without tea? How did it exist? I am glad I was not born before tea!"

Meg Chittenden is the author of over thirty novels, including the Charlie Plato mystery series and the suspense novel, *More Than You Know*. Visit her at www.mchittenden.com.

THE PROOF IS IN THE PUDDING

Sticky Toffee Pudding

DICK FRANCIS

While attending Malice Domestic XII in May 2000, your trusty cookbook co-authors had a delightful encounter with Felix Francis, son of mystery master Dick Francis. Felix was there to accept the Lifetime Achievement Award on his father's behalf, and he came up to us after a panel on culinary mysteries to say that if we ever put together a second volume he was certain his father would offer up the recipe for a Francis family favorite.

When *A Second Helping of Murder* became a reality, Dick Francis was on the top of our list of potential contributors. Only problem—we had neglected to get contact information and no one seemed to know where we might find Felix. A Yahoo search resulted in nine e-mail addresses for various Felix Francises (who would have imagined there could be so many?), but none led us to the elusive Felix. Momentary despair was assuaged by the indominitable Barbara Peters, who we now realize does indeed know *everyone* in the mystery world. A quick note from Barbara and the Francis family recipe arrived promptly in our inbox.

Now that Dick Francis has retired from mystery writing, his legion of fans must content themselves with rereading his prodigious backlist. Maybe a few helpings of this tasty treat will help ease the pain.

What goes in:

White bread   Butter
Milk   Golden syrup*
Vanilla essence

What to do:

Cut very thick (at least an inch thick) slices of white bread (one per person unless you are *very* hungry). Remove crusts. Place the milk in a shallow dish and add a couple of drops of vanilla essence. Place the bread in the milk so that it soaks up the liquid—allow to sit in the milk for 10 minutes or so, to become soft and fully saturated. Place some butter and some golden syrup in a pan, and heat, so that the butter and syrup become mixed and runny. Use a fish slice (spatula) to carefully lift the milk-soaked bread into the pan. Simmer until the liquid caramel toffee begins to form. Turn the bread over and baste with syrup sauce. Simmer until brown—the longer the simmer, the thicker the toffee. Lift out and allow to cool for 5 minutes. Eat.

Beware: The caramel toffee is very hot when simmering. You must allow it to cool for some minutes before eating.

*Helpful hint: If you don't have a British import shop nearby, an easy substitute for golden syrup is light corn syrup.

Dick Francis is the author of more than thirty best-selling mysteries set in the horse racing world, including *Straight, Dead Cert,* and *Come To Grief.*

Heavenly Lemon Mystery
MIGNON F. BALLARD

*T*his is my mother's recipe and was always a favorite of mine growing up. Since my character, Augusta Goodnight, guardian angel "temp," spends a lot of time in the kitchen—aside from her sleuthing duties—it would certainly be in her "comfort" collection. Not recommended for dieters, this dessert is even better topped with sweetened whipped cream, but it's very good without it.

> 2 tablespoons butter or margarine
> 1 cup sugar
> 4 tablespoons flour
> ⅛ teaspoon salt
> Juice and grated rind of one lemon
> 3 eggs (beat yolks and whites separately)
> 1 ½ cups milk

Cream the butter, add the sugar, and mix well. Add the flour, salt, rind, and juice of lemon. Stir in the egg yolks mixed with milk, then fold in the beaten whites. Pour into a baking dish, and set the dish in a shallow pan of hot water. Bake in a 350 degree oven for 45 minutes.

Serves 6 normal people or 4 lemon lovers.

Mignon F. Ballard's mysteries featuring chocolate-loving heavenly detective Augusta Goodnight include *the Angel Whispered Danger, Shadow of an Angel,* and *Angel at Troublesome Creek.*

Ruby Bee's Rhubarb Pie

JOAN HESS

*R*uby Bee keeps trying to convince her daughter Arly that the only way to win a man is to learn how to prepare tasty home-cooked treats. To Ruby Bee's dismay, thus far the only interest Arly has shown in food is eating it.

This is one of her favorites.

3 ½ cups diced rhubarb
½ cup white sugar
1 teaspoon flour
1 9-inch single crust pie shell
¼ cup butter or margarine
½ cup packed brown sugar
½ cup crushed cornflakes
½ cup flour

Combine the first 3 ingredients and put in the pie shell. Melt the butter and combine with the remaining ingredients. Pat down on the top of the pie. Bake at 350 degrees for about 40 minutes. Turn off the oven and leave the pie in it for another hour.

Serve warm with whipped cream or a dollop of vanilla ice cream.

Joan Hess is the author of the Maggody series, including *Muletrain to Maggody* and *Maggody and the Moonbeams.*

Hot Cheese Pie

NANCY TESLER

This pie is hot. I purloined the recipe from the chef at a restaurant on the premises of the ski resort where my family and I used to vacation, and where the latest of my Carrie Carlin series, *Slippery Slopes and Other Deadly Things*, takes place. The chef guarded his recipe as if it were the holy grail itself. Neither feminine wiles nor the pleas of hungry children could worm it out of him. Were we destined to eat garden variety cheese pie for the rest of our lives? Would Carrie allow this mystery to go unsolved? Never!

We began to eat pie—night after night after night. Who worried about calories? Not these sleuths. We would ski them off. We compared notes. What made the pie so fluffy? What gave it its tang? What were those secret ingredients? Cream—heavy or sour? Let's try both. Let's go for lemon juice instead of vanilla. Egg whites, lots of them, beaten till stiff as a corpse.

I went home and practiced. And practice made almost perfect. The following is melt-in-your-mouth delicious and pretty close to the original. That recipe, I'm afraid, the chef will take to his grave.

The texture of this pie is as light and fluffy as fresh powder falling on the slopes on which Carrie skis in her latest adventure. Topped with meringue and served hot right from the oven, its peaks are reminiscent of the ice-tipped mountain tops where the hair-raising climax of the book takes place.

Crust

> 1 cup graham cracker crumbs
> ¼ to ½ cup sugar (depending on your sweet tooth)
> 1 to 2 lumps butter or margarine
> 1 teaspoon cinnamon (optional)
> A few crushed walnuts (optional)

Preheat the oven to 400 degrees. Grease a spring form pan.

Mix all the ingredients together. Press the graham cracker mixture into bottom of the pan.

Pie

> 2 pounds Philadelphia cream cheese
> 2 tablespoons margarine or butter
> 2 tablespoons flour
> ½ cup heavy cream
> 6 egg whites
> 4 egg yolks
> ¾ cup sugar
> Juice of 1 large lemon
> ¼ cup sugar
> ¼ teaspoon cream of tartar
> ½ cup pint sour cream

Melt the butter. When the butter has melted add the flour. Make a roux. In a separate pan bring the cream to a boil. Add the boiling cream slowly to the butter and flour mixture. Mix until not lumpy. Simmer for 1 minute. Remove from the heat.

In a large bowl beat the sugar, cheese and egg yolks together for 10 minutes with an electric mixer. Add the lemon juice. Slowly fold in the hot cream mixture.

Beat 4 egg whites till stiff. Fold into the yolk mixture. Pour into the crust in the pan.

Turn down the oven to 375 degrees and bake for three-quarters of an hour.

Beat the 2 remaining egg whites until stiff. Add the sugar and cream of tartar. Fold in the sour cream. When the pie is done, top with this meringue, and bake 2 to 4 minutes. Serve warm.

Nancy Tesler's "Other Deadly Things" mystery series, featuring stress-reduction biofeedback specialist and single mom Carrie Carlin, includes *Slippery Slopes and Other Deadly Things, Pink Balloons and Other Deadly Things,* and *Sharks, Jellyfish and Other Deadly Things.* To learn more, visit www.nancytesler.com.

Levinson's Easy Chocolate Mousse Pie
ROBERT S. LEVINSON

*F*or all those chocoholics out there, this one's for you.

It's a cinch to concoct—especially if all you have to do (as I do religiously whenever I'm in the kitchen) is stand to one side and watch your spouse work the magic—and it's a dream going down.

Levinson's Easy Chocolate Mousse Pie is a dessert I stumbled into a few years ago, when a silly ol' operation on my throat resulted in limitations on what I could eat, but no restrictions whatsoever on the calorie count.

I liked the dessert so much, in fact, that I made it the favorite of Neil Gulliver, who co-stars with his ex-spouse, Stevie Marriner, in my series of "Affair" novels. The basic problem there, however: sex symbol Stevie is so diet conscious—and so much the chocoholic herself—that she won't make Levinson's Easy Chocolate Mousse Pie for Neil.

Fortunately, Neil is always welcome at the Levinson abode, and my wife, Sandra, is never reluctant to have a slice or two ready and waiting for him.

¾ cup milk	8 ounces chocolate (bittersweet is good)
30 large marshmallows	15 ounces Cool Whip

Pour the milk into a large microwave-safe mixing bowl. Add the marshmallows and chocolate (broken into small pieces).

Microwave 4 to 5 minutes. Watch it, it can spill over. Stir to mix and cool completely.

Add the Cool Whip. Pour into the chocolate crumb crust (recipe follows).

Chill until firm.

Crumb Crust

15 to 20 Oreos or 15 Famous Chocolate Cookies

Process the cookies into crumbs in processor or blender. If using Famous Chocolate Cookies, mix crumbs with ¼ pound melted butter to form the crust.

Press the crumb mix into a deep pie dish.

Microwave for 30 seconds. Cool before filling.

Variations:
- Add whole chunks of chocolate to final mix.
- Add nuts to final mix.
- Make as a mousse, spoon into individual dishes, and garnish with whipped cream or chocolate shavings.
- Add extract or coffee for different flavor.

Robert Levinson is the best-selling author of *Hot Paint*, *The John Lennon Affair*, and *The James Dean Affair*. Visit him at www.robertlevinson.com.

J.B.'s Cinnamon Rolls

APRIL HENRY

$\mathscr{I}$ work full-time, I write a book a year, and I've got a kid. How does one do it all? Often, one doesn't. Or screws up. There was the time I was making my famous cinnamon rolls and grabbed the chili powder instead of the cinnamon. Did you know you can wash dough?

These cinnamon rolls come from a recipe passed on by my mom (don't tell!). I've blind taste-tested them against "Nikki's Cinnamon Buns from Heaven," and "Big Gorgeous Cinnamon Rolls." These rolls won, hands down. Interesting enough, other recipes use what would seem to be more high-end ingredients, such as all butter instead of shortening, or all milk instead of a combination of water and milk.

Though the recipe does not appear in the book, these are the cinnamon rolls J.B. cooks in *Square in the Face*, the follow-up to *Circles of Confusion*.

For the Dough

½ cup warm water
2 packages yeast (if using rapid rise, follow package directions)
½ cup milk, scalded and cooled to lukewarm
5 cups flour, plus more for kneading
½ cup shortening
½ cup sugar
1 teaspoon salt
2 eggs

For the Filling

¼ cup melted butter (½ stick)
¾ cup sugar
1 ½ tablespoons cinnamon
¾ cups chopped walnuts or pecans (optional)

For an Optional Cream Cheese Frosting

6 ounces cream cheese, softened
1 ½ cups powdered sugar
1 teaspoons vanilla
1 ½ to 2 tablespoons milk

Mix the water, yeast, and milk together. In a large separate bowl, mix 4 cups of flour, sugar and salt. Add the liquids and shortening. Stir in the eggs. Add enough flour for dough to hold together. With floured hands, knead for 8 to 10 minutes on a floured surface until the dough is smooth and springy, like a baby's butt. Add a little more flour as needed. Turn in a greased bowl, and let rise in a warm place, covered, until doubled, about 1 to 1 ½ hours. Punch down, let rise again until nearly double, about 45 minutes.

Roll out into a rectangle about ½ inch thick. Top with the melted butter. Mix the sugar and cinnamon together, and sprinkle on the melted butter. Sprinkle with nuts, if desired. Roll up to form a log, jelly-roll fashion, and pinch ends together to seal. Cut with dental floss or doubled string into 1 ½-inch slices.

Grease the bottom of one 13-by-9-inch baking pan and one 8-inch square pan with butter, and sprinkle a little sugar in each pan. Place the cinnamon roll slices close together. Cover, let rise again until about double, about 45 minutes.

Bake at 375 degrees until tops begin to brown, about 15 minutes. Let cool slightly.

If desired, frost with cream cheese frosting: Beat the cream cheese and powdered sugar in a bowl until smooth. Add the vanilla and enough milk to achieve drizzling consistency. Drizzle frosting across the top of each bun.

Note: Without the cinnamon/sugar/butter filling, this also makes a nice dinner roll.

April Henry is the author of the Claire Montrose series, which includes *Heart-Shaped Box*, and the suspense thriller *Learning to Fly*. Learn more at AprilHenryMysteries.com.

Dairy Farmer Ruth's Honey-Dipped Doughnuts

NANCY MEANS WRIGHT

Along with gulps of strong hot coffee, Ruth's doughnuts keep her fueled for the hard work of milking and sleuthing. She extracts honey from hives supplied by a beekeeper friend (see *Stolen Honey*), and buttermilk from her beloved cows. Her would-be lover, Colm Hanna, adores her doughnuts. He leaves her kitchen with a honey of a mustache!

> 1 ½ cups all-purpose flour
> 1 egg
> ¼ teaspoon ground nutmeg
> ½ cup buttermilk
> 1 ½ cups honey
> 1 tablespoon shortening
> 1 teaspoon baking powder
> ½ teaspoon baking soda
> ½ teaspoon salt
> Extra virgin olive oil
> At least 1 extra cup of honey for dipping
> Deep-fat thermometer

Combine ¾ cup of flour, egg, buttermilk, honey, shortening, baking powder and soda, salt, and nutmeg. Beat the mixture on low speed until blended. Beat one more minute on medium speed.

Stir in the remaining ¾ cup flour. Refrigerate the dough one hour. Roll the dough on a board with a floured rolling pin to ½-inch thick. Cut the dough into rings with a floured 3 ½- inch doughnut cutter. Press the "holes" and other trimmings together; roll and cut to use up all the dough.

Heat 3 inches of olive oil in a 3-quart pan over medium heat to 370 degrees on a deep-fat thermometer. Fry the doughnuts in hot oil; turn with a slotted spoon as they rise to the surface. Keep turning until golden (4 to 6 minutes). Drain on paper towels.

Makes about 1 dozen doughnuts. For dipping, pour 2 inches of honey into a small saucepan and bring to a boil. When the doughnuts are removed from the fryer and drained, poke a few holes in their sides with a toothpick. Place each doughnut in the boiling honey for about 15 seconds, then turn over and dip the other side. Transfer to a rack placed over a piece of wax paper. Repeat with the remaining doughnuts, adding more honey as needed. Serve the doughnuts when the dip has dried.

Feisty Vermont farmer Ruth appears in the mystery novels of Nancy Means Wright, including *Mad Season*, *Poison Apples*, and *Stolen Honey*.

Bailey's Irish Cream Bread-and-Butter Pudding

KRIS NERI

*B*y now a great many mystery readers know I made mention of a yummy recipe, Bailey's Irish Cream Tiramisú, in my first Tracy Eaton mystery, *Revenge of the Gypsy Queen*. I've handed out thousands of recipe cards for that recipe at signings and through my website (www.krisneri.com). But what nobody knows is that I created a prior Bailey's recipe for use in that book, but which I deemed to be too homey for the Eaton table. However, this one is equally delicious and even more comforting. It's one of my all-time favorites.

4 large slices French bread (or 6 to 8 small slices)	3 eggs, slightly beaten
2 tablespoons butter, softened	⅓ cup granulated sugar
⅓ cup light brown sugar, packed	1 teaspoon vanilla extract
½ teaspoon cinnamon	Dash salt
⅓ cup chopped walnuts	½ cup Bailey's Irish Cream liqueur
¼ cup semi-sweet chocolate chips	2 cups milk, scalded

Heat oven to 350 degrees. Liberally butter a 1 ½-quart casserole container. Toast the bread slices lightly. Spread one side of each slice with butter. Mix together the brown sugar and cinnamon. Sprinkle the buttered surfaces with brown sugar and cinnamon mixture. Reserving ¼ each of the nuts and chocolate chips, sprinkle the remaining chopped nuts and chocolate chip pieces on the buttered/sugared surfaces.

Put the buttered/sugared sides together to form 2 large sandwiches. Trim the crusts. Cut each sandwich into 4 fingers. Arrange the fingers in a single layer in the casserole dish. Sprinkle with the remaining nuts and chocolate chips.

Blend together the eggs, granulated sugar, vanilla, and salt. Stir in the Bailey's Irish Cream liqueur. Slowly stir in the hot milk. Pour over the sandwich fingers in the casserole dish. Place the casserole dish in a pan of very hot water, 1-inch deep. Bake 65 to 70 minutes, or until a toothpick inserted in center comes out clean.

Serve warm with commercial or homemade whipped cream, or with Bailey's hard sauce (recipe follows).

Bailey's Hard Sauce

½ cup butter	1 cup confectioner's sugar
½ teaspoon vanilla extract	3 tablespoons Bailey's Irish Cream.

Soften the butter by bringing to room temperature. Cream the butter and beat in confectioner's sugar. Beat until very light. Add the vanilla and continue to beat. Beat in the Bailey's. Serve immediately by drizzling over warm bread pudding.

Makes 6 to 8 servings.

Kris Neri writes the Tracy Eaton mysteries, *Revenge of the Gypsy Queen*, *Dem Bones' Revenge* and the forthcoming *Revenge for Old Times' Sake*.

Accidental Bakewell Pudding

STEPHEN BOOTH

$\mathcal{L}$ate at night, after a long spell of duty, a hard-working police officer is bound to start thinking about food. There's a scene in *Dancing with the Virgins* where Detective Constable Ben Cooper stops on his way home to peer into the window of a baker's shop, and imagines the food that is usually on display there. Just writing this passage made me feel hungry!

During the day the window was full of pastries and cheeses—apricot white Stilton, homity pies, Peak pasties, and enormous high-baked pork pies. Cooper came down as often as he could at lunch-times if he was in town. He was happy to queue with the tourists and listen to the assistants explaining one more time that Bakewell tarts should be called Bakewell puddings.

Of course, those local delicacies named after the English Peak District town of Bakewell are tarts really. But no British tradition is complete without its eccentric name—and its eccentric origins.

According to legend, Bakewell Pudding was created by accident. It was around 1860 when an inexperienced kitchen maid at the Rutland Arms hotel in Bakewell is said to have misunderstood the instructions for making strawberry tart. The result of her culinary disaster proved so popular with customers that it was patented and is still being sold to tourists today, right across the street from the hotel at The Old Original Bakewell Pudding Shop.

In fact, those very first appreciative customers may well have been tourists themselves. Visitors to the Rutland Arms included Jane Austen, who stayed there while writing *Pride and Prejudice*.

Try the treat that made DC Ben Cooper's mouth water:

Short Crust

> 8 ounces plain flour
> Pinch salt
> 4 ounces margarine
> 3 tablespoons cold water

Sift the flour and salt into a bowl. Rub in the margarine until the mixture resembles fine breadcrumbs. Add the water, and bind to a firm but pliable dough.

Pudding

> 6 to 8 ounces short crust pastry
> Flour (for coating use)
> 3 ounces butter
> 3 ounces caster sugar
> 3 egg yolks, lightly beaten
> 2 egg whites
> $\frac{1}{4}$ teaspoon almond essence (or extract), or almond oil if you have it
> 3 tablespoons firm set strawberry jam

Preheat oven to 400 degrees. Place a flat baking sheet in to warm up (the bottom of the pie needs extra heat to cook the pastry). Roll the pastry out and use to line a very well-floured pie plate about 7 inches across and 1 inch deep, with a tiny lip all the way round. Traditionally it should be an oval shape, but it won't change the flavor. Spread the jam thinly on the bottom of the pastry.

Beat (cream) together butter and sugar until light and fluffy, and work in the egg yolks and almond essence bit by bit. In a separate clean, dry bowl, whisk the egg whites with a clean, dry whisk until the mix is in soft peaks, then beat into the butter and sugar mix. The mixture should be thick but pourable. Pour the mixture into the pastry, and place in the oven on the pre-heated baking sheet.

After about 15 minutes, check the pie to see if the top is browning. If it is getting quite dark, reduce the heat down to 350 degrees. Bake for a further 20 to 25 minutes. After this time, the mix should be risen up and dark on top. It won't be thoroughly solid, but it's actually meant to be slightly soft.

Allow to cool slightly. The top will sink a bit, but it's meant to.

Serve warm, with cream or ice cream.

Stephen Booth is the author of *Black Dog*, *Dancing With Virgins* and *Blood On The Tongue*, and a double Barry Award Winner for Best British crime Novel of 2000 and 2001. Visit him at www.stephen-booth.com.

Kick Keswick's Priceless Pineapple Upside-Down Cake

MARNE DAVIS KELLOGG

Name: Katherine Day Keswick (aka "Kick")
Occupation: Retired Executive Assistant at Ballantine & Company
    Auctioneer, Ltd., London
Actual Occupation: Retired Jewel Thief: The notorious Shamrock Burglar
Age: Forty-something, but never verified
Aspiration: Remain in Provence, cooking beautiful meals
    (including this scrumptious dessert) and living anonymously
Inspiration: Doris Day
Greatest Wish: Privacy
Greatest Strengths: Precision and taste
Biggest Problem: Staying one step ahead of the authorities

Preheat oven to 350 degrees.

½ cup melted butter	1 can sliced pineapple, drained
1 cup packed brown sugar	

Melt the butter in a skillet. Add the brown sugar, and cook gently until melted. Remove the skillet from the heat, and place the pineapple slices flat on the melted butter and sugar, starting with the center. You might have a couple left over. Set aside.

1 cup *sifted* cake flour	1 teaspoon baking powder

Resift the flour with the baking powder.

4 egg yolks	1 tablespoon dark rum
1 teaspoon melted butter	*or* 1 teaspoon vanilla

In a separate bowl, beat the yolks. Add the melted butter and rum.

4 egg whites

In a large bowl, beat the whites until stiff and they hold firm peaks (you might want to add ½ teaspoon of cream of tartar).

1 cup *sifted* sugar

Beat in the sugar, 1 tablespoon at a time. Add the yolk mixture. Fold in the flour mixture ¼ cup at a time.

Pour the batter on top of the pineapples and brown sugar, and bake for 45 minutes. Reverse onto a cake plate and sprinkle with a little more rum. Can be served hot or cold, and with or without whipped or ice cream.

Anti-heroine Kick Keswick appears in Marne Davis Kellogg's best-selling *Brilliant* and forthcoming *Priceless*.

Skye's the Limit Chocolate Rum Cake

(The Closest Thing to Heaven in Scumble River)
DENISE SWANSON

*L*ike my sleuth, Skye Denison, this recipe is slightly over the top. In Skye's fourth adventure, *Murder of a Snake in the Grass*, her ex-fiancé comes to Scumble River to try and win her back. He has no more of chance of doing this than anyone trying to resist a second piece of this cake.

Many years ago I made this cake for an ER nurse and she brought it to the hospital to share with her fellow workers. Later that day I got a call asking if they could send the Lifeline helicopter to pick up another one. Yes, it's that good!

4 squares unsweetened chocolate	1 cup sifted cake flour
¾ cup milk	1 teaspoon baking powder
¼ cup rum	4 eggs, separated
1 teaspoon vanilla	2 cups sugar

Lightly grease 2 8-inch round cake pans. Preheat the oven to 350 degrees.

Place the unsweetened chocolate, milk, rum, and vanilla in a small saucepan. Cook over low heat, stirring constantly until blended (do not microwave). Remove from heat and cool to room temperature.

Sift together the flour and baking powder. Put aside.

Beat the egg whites until stiff. Put aside. Beat the egg yolks in a large mixing bowl, gradually adding sugar. Continue beating until thick. Stir in the flour/baking powder mixture alternating with the chocolate mixture. Fold the stiff egg whites gently into batter.

Bake 30 minutes, or until toothpick comes out clean. Cool 10 minutes in the pans then remove and cool completely.

Frosting

2 squares melted unsweetened chocolate	2 tablespoons milk
½ cup softened butter	2 tablespoons rum
1 pound powdered sugar	1 teaspoon vanilla

Beat the butter, gradually adding melted chocolate. Stir in powdered sugar. Add the milk, rum, and vanilla. Beat until smooth.

Denise Swanson is the author of the Scumble River Mystery series featuring school psychologist-sleuth Skye Denison and set in rural Illinois. Her first book, *Murder of a Small-Town Honey*, was nominated for an Agatha, her second, *Murder of a Sweet Old Lady*, was nominated for the Mary Higgins Clark Award, and her third, *Murder of a Sleeping Beauty*, was an IMBA bestseller. Visit www.DeniseSwanson.com.

Texas Cake

SUSAN MCBRIDE

The first in my new "Debutante Dropout" series, *Blue Blood*, has Andrea Kendricks back in Dallas after living in Chicago. Despite appearances, her coming home had less to do with guilt about abandoning her widowed mother, socialite Cissy Blevins Kendricks, and more to do with the family recipe for Texas Cake. This delicious dessert is nearly as big as the Lone Star State, and so sweet and moist you'll feel like you've died and gone to heaven.

2 cups flour
2 cups sugar
1 teaspoon salt
½ teaspoon cinnamon
¼ stick margarine
½ cup lard
3 tablespoons cocoa
1 cup water
2 eggs
1 teaspoon baking soda
1 teaspoon vanilla
½ cup buttermilk

Put the flour, sugar, salt, and cinnamon in a mixing bowl.

Separately, bring to a boil the margarine, lard, cocoa, vanilla, and water. Pour the melted mixture into a well made in the flour mixture. Mix together and then add the eggs, baking soda and buttermilk.

Pour into a greased jelly roll pan and spread evenly. Bake at 350 degrees for 20 minutes. Remove from the oven and ice immediately with these combined ingredients:

1 stick margarine
3 tablespoons cocoa
6 tablespoons cream

1 tablespoon vanilla
½ cup chopped pecans
1 pound powdered sugar

Heat the margarine, cocoa, cream, and vanilla, but do not boil. Stir until mixed and then pour over powdered sugar in a bowl, mixing thoroughly. Then add the nuts. Pour the icing over cake warm from oven and spread evenly. Let cool just a bit, then enjoy!

Susan McBride is the author of Blue Blood, the first in "The Debutante Dropout Series." and the Maggie Ryan books, *And Then She Was Gone* and *Overkill*. Her website can be found at http://susanmcbride.com.

Sweeney St. George's Gravestone Cake

SARAH STEWART TAYLOR

$\mathcal{M}$y detective Sweeney St. George is an art historian who specializes in gravestone art. She loves gravestones as much as I love making this wonderful walnut mocha cake. It's surprisingly easy, yet people are always impressed by it. The cake itself is light, almost soufflé-like, yet rich with pulverized walnuts, and the grainy texture looks remarkably like a granite headstone. The frosting is rich, fluffy mocha whipped cream. The recipe is courtesy of my friend Jennifer Hauck, who takes my author photos. Enjoy!

Cake

1 cup walnuts
2 tablespoons flour
2 ½ teaspoons baking powder
4 eggs
¾ cup sugar

Frosting

1 teaspoon instant coffee
1 cup heavy cream
⅓ cup sugar
¼ cup cocoa powder

Grease and flour 2 round cake pans.

In the bowl of a food processor, combine the nuts, flour and baking powder. Add the eggs and sugar, and process for a few minutes before pouring the batter into the pans. Don't worry if it doesn't look like much in the pans. It will rise a lot. Bake at 350 degrees for 20 to 25 minutes. Cool completely.

Just before you're ready to serve the cake, make the frosting. It might be a good idea to make double if you really like chocolate and coffee! Dissolve the instant coffee in the cream. Beat until slightly thickened, then add the sugar and cocoa, and beat until it's the right consistency for spreading. Slather the frosting inside and outside the cake and serve.

O' Artful Death is the first in Sarah Stewart Taylor's series featuring art historian and gravestone expert Sweeney St. George. Her website can be found at www.SarahStewartTaylor.com.

Old-Fashioned Blackberry Cake

JEFFREY MARKS

*T*his is the type of cake that would have been brought to Widow Halley's home after her husband's funeral in *A Good Soldier*.

> 1 cup buttermilk
> 1 teaspoon soda
> 1 cup sugar
> ¾ cup butter
> 4 eggs
> 1 ½ cups fresh blackberries (or 1 cup of seedless blackberry preserves)
> 2 cups flour
> 1 teaspoon *each:* cinnamon, allspice & nutmeg
> Pinch salt

Put the soda in the buttermilk and mix well. Cream the sugar and butter. Add beaten eggs and fruit or preserves; then remainder of ingredients.

Bake at 375 degrees in three 9-inch cake pans until a fork or toothpick comes out clean.

Cream Cheese Frosting

> 1 8-ounce package cream cheese
> ½ cup butter (1 stick)
> 1 16-ounce package confectioner's sugar
> 1 tablespoon cream
> 1 teaspoon vanilla

Cream the cheese and butter; add sugar, vanilla, and cream; mix well and apply to the cake, between the layers and then over the entire cake.

Jeffrey Marks is the Edgar-nominated author of the US Grant mystery series, which includes *A Good Soldier,* and the editor of *Murder, Mystery and Malone.*

Orange Slice Cake

MARLIS DAY

*T*his holiday dessert, passed on to me by an art teacher in Chicago almost four decades ago, has become a tradition in our family. However, when people see it for the first time, it is necessary to yell, "IT'S NOT A FRUITCAKE!" Unfortunately, it seems that many people loathe fruitcake and will hesitate to try it unless forewarned. This cake is rich and moist and needs no icing. When wrapped, it ages to perfection and may be eaten as dessert or breakfast bread for a week. It is excellent with coffee on a cold wintry day, especially while reading a mystery. (See list at bottom.)

Since the third Margo Brown mystery, *The Curriculum Murders*, takes place over the holidays, it was essential to include the festive cake. As Margo contemplates the current crime (small matter of a serial killer stalking and killing his former teachers), she chops and dices the ingredients for the traditional treat. Duly proud of her Christmas cake, she slides pieces into colorful tins and presents them as gifts. Because amateur sleuth Margo must juggle wifery, parenting, and sleuthing, it is no surprise that she often grasps insights into the crimes as she cooks and bakes for her family. The surprise comes later in the story when one of the recipients of the holiday cake tries to kill her. Ooops.

Sift together and set aside:

> 3 ½ cups flour and ½ teaspoon salt

Combine and set aside:

> 1 pound chopped orange slice candy
> 8 ounces chopped dates
> 2 cups walnut pieces
> 1 cup coconut (3 ½ ounces)

Add ½ cup of the flour mix and mix well.

In a separate bowl, cream until light and fluffy:

> 1 cup butter   1 ½ to 2 cups sugar

Add 4 eggs, beating well after each.

Combine 1 teaspoon baking soda and ½ cup buttermilk.

Add the buttermilk and flour mix to creamed mixture alternately.

Blend well; add the candy mix. Put into greased 9-by-13-inch pan.

Bake 1 ½ hours at 300 degrees.

Respectfully submitted by Marlis Day, author of the Margo Brown Mysteries: *Why Johnny Died*, *Death of a Hoosier Schoolmaster*, and the forthcoming *The Curriculum Murders*.

Myra's Real New York Cheesecake
LARRY KARP

Thomas Purdue and Broadway Schwartz like to stop at a deli to touch base over a piece of cheesecake. New York cheesecake. *Real* New York cheesecake. Oh, do I envy them. I live in a lovely city, full of nice people and great coffee, but don't ever order "New York Cheesecake" in a Seattle restaurant. What you'll get is a chiffony confection that melts away practically before it's in your mouth. *Real* New York Cheesecake sticks to your teeth like peanut butter laced with superglue; you're still enjoying it half an hour later.

So, here you go. Enjoy the McCoy: Myra's *Real* New York Cheesecake. (Myra is my wife, who swears she is not the model for Sarah Purdue). To the best of my knowledge, no one has died as the result of baking or eating this cake. However, we take no responsibility for lost fillings, overloaded bathroom scales, abnormal treadmill tests, or sprained or dislocated elbows from lifting the cake from the oven.

Crust

1 ½ cups graham-cracker crumbs
3 tablespoons sugar

1 teaspoon ground cinnamon
¼ cup unsalted butter, melted

Filling

3 8-ounce packages cream cheese,
   or 2 packages cream cheese and
   1 package Neufchatel,
   at room temperature
1 ¼ cups sugar

6 large eggs, separated
2 cups sour cream
⅓ cup flour
1 tablespoon vanilla
1 tablespoon lemon juice

Generously grease a 9-by-3-inch spring form pan with butter. Place the pan in the center of a 12-inch square of foil, and press the foil around the sides of pan. Mix the graham-cracker crumbs, sugar, cinnamon, and melted butter until well blended. Press into the bottom and sides of the pan. Chill while making filling.

With a mixer on low, beat the cream cheese until soft. Gradually beat in the sugar until light and fluffy. Beat in the egg yolks, one at a time, until well blended. Stir in the sour cream, flour, vanilla, and lemon juice until smooth. Beat the egg whites until they hold stiff peaks. Fold into the cheese mixture until blended. (Do not beat in). Pour into the pan.

Bake in a 350 degree oven for 1 hour and 15 minutes, or until the top is golden. Then turn off the oven heat, and allow cake to cool in the oven for 1 hour. *This Step Is Critical:* Remove the cake from the oven, and cool to room temperature on a wire rack. Chill overnight before serving.

Larry Karp writes the Thomas Purdue Music Box mystery series, which includes *The Music Box Murders, Scamming The Birdman,* and *The Midnight Special.* Find out more at www.larrykarp.com.

Appleton Loaf

KATHY LYNN EMERSON

*T*he recipe is a personal favorite, renamed for my series character, who has found poison in a variety of dishes in the books and short stories in the series. There is no poison in this one.

> 1 stick margarine
> 1 cup sugar (or Splenda)
> Dash of salt
> 1 teaspoon vanilla
> 2 eggs (or ½ cup egg substitute)
> 2 cups flour
> 2 teaspoons baking powder
> 2 tablespoons evaporated milk
> 2 cups apple chunks, whatever size you prefer

Cream the margarine, then add the sugar, vanilla, and a dash of salt. Beat until fluffy. Add eggs and beat well. Add the flour, baking powder, and evaporated milk (you can substitute skim milk but evaporated is better). Beat batter well. It will be very thick. Fold in the apple chunks. Pack batter into a well-greased glass loaf pan.

Bake at 350 degrees for 1 hour and 15 minutes. Cool on a rack for 10 minutes before removing from pan.

Serve in thick slices.

Kathy Lynn Emerson writes the Face Down series, featuring Susanna, Lady Appleton, a sixteenth century gentlewoman, herbalist, and sleuth, which includes *Face Down in the Marrow-Bone Pie*. She is launching a second historical mystery series featuring 19th century newspaper columnist Diana Spaulding with *Deadlier than the Pen*. Her website is www.kathylynnemerson.com.

Cook's Gingerbread

We all know food has been used as a means to cause harm or death in countless thrillers, mysteries, and even fairy tales (remember Snow White?). And that many a plot has thickened while a meal was being served.

But in Agatha Christie's *Sleeping Murder,* a recipe is used as the method of obtaining information pertaining to the disappearance of Major Halliday's wife. Knowing the cook could shed some light on the disappearance, the unflappable Miss Marple expresses her desire for a few good recipes (including cook's delectable gingerbread, served during her visit at the Halliday home) as a ruse to procure the cook's address so she may question her. *"I so love a good gingerbread."*

Although Miss Marple solved the crime, she never had a chance to make the gingerbread…but here's your opportunity to savor some made the British way. (Keep in mind: making the gingerbread in advance and keeping it in a closed tin or wrapped in foil for a couple of days improves the flavor.)

8 ounces flour
½ teaspoon salt
1 teaspoon bicarbonate of soda (aka baking soda)
3 teaspoons ground ginger
1 teaspoon ground cinnamon
3 ounces white cooking fat
4 ounces soft brown sugar
3 ounces black treacle
3 ounces golden syrup (available at British food import stores)
2 eggs
6 tablespoons milk
2 ounces sultanas (pale yellow, seedless raisins)
2 ounces preserved (crystallized or candied) ginger, chopped
1 ounce candied fruit peel, chopped
2 ounces blanched almonds, flaked

Sift the flour, bicarbonate of soda, ginger, and cinnamon into a bowl and set aside.

Cut the fat up into a saucepan and add the sugar, treacle, and golden syrup. Warm gently over low heat until the fat has just melted and the ingredients are blended. Remove from the heat, and set aside until the hand can be held comfortably against the sides of the pan. Lightly mix the eggs and milk, and stir into the contents of the saucepan. Mix together thoroughly.

Pour the egg and syrup mixture into the center of the flour, and mix with a wooden spoon until smooth and glossy. Stir in the sultanas, ginger, and candied peel. Pour into an 8-inch square cake pan, which has been greased and lined at the bottom with greased paper. Sprinkle with flaked almonds.

Place in the center of a moderately low oven, 325 degrees, and bake for 1 hour. Do not open the oven during the first 40 minutes or the cake may subside in the middle.

Remove from the oven when time is completed. Turn onto a rack and let cool.

Cut into 24 squares and serve…with or without fresh cream.

Invasion of the Body Snatchers Chocolate Pod Cake
LOU ALLIN

*I*n Northern Ontario, the Nickel Capital of the World, where it's -25 degrees centigrade as I write this, food is important! My mid-forties sleuth takes refuge in concocting rich and delicious meals to fuel up against blizzards. This recipe is from *Blackflies Are Murder*. Realtor Belle Palmer, like her gardening neighbors, often lets a zucchini or two escape her eagle eye. The resulting ball-bat-sized vegetable shouldn't be wasted, even if it does resemble one of the alien pods in the memorable film *Invasion of the Body Snatchers* (watching Turner Classics is her favorite indoor pastime). Best turn it into an edible delight before it takes human form.

2 ½ cups flour
½ cup cocoa
2 ½ teaspoons baking powder
1 ½ teaspoons baking soda
1 teaspoon salt
1 teaspoon cinnamon
¾ cup soft butter
2 cups sugar
3 eggs
½ cup milk
1 teaspoon vanilla
2 teaspoons grated lemon rind
2 cups grated zucchini
1 cup chopped pecans (optional)

Mix the dry ingredients in a large bowl and set aside. Beat together the butter, sugar, and eggs. In a separate bowl combine the milk, vanilla, lemon rind, zucchini, and pecans, if desired.

Mix all 3 sets of ingredients together in the large bowl and beat well.

Bake in greased loaf pans at 350 degrees for 1 hour.

Makes 3 small loaves or 2 large ones.

Lou Allin's Belle Palmer series includes *Northern Winters Are Murder*, *Blackflies Are Murder*, and *Bush Poodles Are Murder*. Learn more at www.louallin.com.

Deathly Sweet Chocolate and Caramel Cake
GAY TOTL KINMAN

This recipe holds a special significance for me. I picked out a recipe that was as gooey, caloric and rich as possible—a fantasy recipe. I don't make or eat desserts usually but if I did, either the ingredients of this one is what I would want—caramel and chocolate. I've made this cake three times. Not wanting my husband to keel over with clogged arteries, but wanting to be sure that the concoction was edible, as I had revised the recipe, I took each of the batches to the Huntington Library on successive Thursday mornings and left them in the Footnote (the coffee break room). When I took a break at 10:30, the glass dish was lined only with sticky crumbs. No one died, or even had a heart attack. Success!

The recipe result is a great way to kill someone who loves desserts but already has clogged arteries. "Nothing is too good for you, sweetie. A little second helping can't possibly make a difference!" Or in the case of my husband, "Oh, no, darling, there aren't any sunflower seeds in it. Here have a second helping." I've killed someone with food in a story, but not with this particular dish.

>   1 German chocolate cake mix
>   2 cups softened caramels
>   1 cup sweetened condensed milk
>   1 stick margarine
>   1 cup chocolate chips
>   1 cup coarsely chopped pecans

Grease and flour a 9-by-13-inch glass dish.

Prepare the cake mix according to directions. Pour ½ the batter (2 ½ cups) into the dish, and bake at 325 degrees for 30 minutes.

Melt the caramels, milk, and margarine in the microwave on high, about 7 minutes. Pour the melted mixture over the baked portion of cake. Sprinkle the chocolate chips and pecans evenly. Pour the remaining uncooked batter on top, and bake at 325 degrees for 50 minutes. Let cool before cutting.

Gay Totl Kinman is the author of the gothic novel *Castle Reiner*, set in 1899, as well as a children's mystery series featuring Alison Leigh Powers, Super Sleuth, in *The Secret of the Strange Staircase* and *The Mystery of the Missing Miniature Books*. Her website can be found at http://gaykinman.com.

Kentucky Blackberry Jam Cake with Brown Sugar Icing

E. JOAN SIMS

My grandmother made a delicious cake using jam from the blackberries my grandfather picked on the back of our farm. She added chopped walnuts from our own trees, then placed a walnut half square in the middle of the brown sugar icing on top. Grandmother was not the adventurous type—preferring the rocker on her front porch to an aisle seat on the Concorde, but one year she made a seven minute white icing and colored it with a generous dollop of her luscious jam. She got a standing ovation from her family when she carried that beautiful lavender cake into the dining room. Her recipe was hard to follow—a pinch of this, a smidgen of that, and butter the size of an egg! This is a modern version that I don't think she would mind. Don't get upset if it cracks or falls a little in the middle—this is a homey cake, as comfortable and forgiving as your own grandmother's lap.

    1 box spice cake mix (I use Duncan Hines)
    3 large eggs
    ⅓ cup vegetable oil
    ¾ cup seedless blackberry jam
    ½ cup sweet applesauce
    ½ cup chopped walnuts

Blend all the ingredients except the nuts, and beat with an electric mixer on medium speed for 3 minutes. Add the nuts, and pour into an oiled and floured 13-by-9-inch cake pan.

Bake at 350 degrees for 35 minutes (or until sides brown and pull away from pan).

Icing

    ½ stick butter
    ½ cup light brown sugar
    ⅓ cup evaporated milk
    ⅛ teaspoon salt
    ½ teaspoon vanilla extract
    2 cups confectioner's sugar

Melt the butter, and stir together with the milk, vanilla, salt, and sugar over a medium heat until blended. Remove from heat and cool 5 minutes. Beat in the confectioner's sugar until well-blended. Pour over the cake and spread out evenly.

Serves 16 small servings.

E. Joan Sims is the author of *Cemetery Silk* and *The Plague Doctor*, both featuring Paisley Sterling. Learn more at www.ejoansims.com.

Double Chocolate Mocha Trifle

LAURA YOUNG

*T*his is just the thing reporter Kate Kelly needs to get her through a day of chasing down clues and bad guys in *Killer Looks*. It has all the important elements—it's fast and easy to make for a single girl with limited culinary skills, and has all the essential "food groups"… coffee, sugar, and lots of chocolate!

> 1 package (18.25 ounces) brownie mix (plus ingredients to make brownies)
> 1 ¾ cups cold milk
> 2 packages white chocolate instant pudding and pie filling
> ¼ cup warm water
> 4 teaspoons instant coffee
> 2 cups thawed frozen Cool Whip
> 3 toffee candy bars, coarsely chopped

Prepare and bake the brownie mix in a 9-by-13-inch pan according to cake-like package directions. Cool completely.

In a batter bowl, whisk the pudding mix into the milk until thickened. Dissolve the coffee in warm water; add to the pudding mixture, mixing well. Fold in the whipped topping. Cut the brownies into 1-inch cubes. Chop the toffee bars. Layer ⅓ of the brownie cubes onto the bottom of a deep bowl. Top with ⅓ of the pudding mixture, pressing lightly, and ⅓ of the chopped toffee. Repeat layers as needed. Chill 30 minutes before serving.

Yields 12 very rich servings. (About 470 calories and 23 grams of fat per serving, but who's counting?)

Laura Young's heroine, travel reporter Kate Kelly, can be found taking an unwanted trip through Virginia—involving mistaken identity, murder, and old family secrets—in *Killer Looks*. In *Otherwise Engaged* she learns that being a bride-to-be involves more than picking out china patterns and battling the in-laws. It might just be the death of her.

Swiss Toblerone Soufflés

MARION MOORE HILL

Oklahoma librarian Juanita Wills can track down an elusive fact or a clever killer, using her own blend of wit, nosiness and independence. But resourceful and cheerful as she usually is, Juanita sometimes feels she's in over her head. Then, she bakes—and eats, of course—"something rich, something chocolate." The soufflé she cooks in *Bookmarked For Murder*, first in a planned "Sassy Librarian" series, is a variation of a recipe I found in *Bon Appetit* magazine years ago and modified.

The base for these soufflées is made with Switzerland's Toblerone chocolate, which contains honey-almond nougat. These desserts can be assembled three days ahead and frozen; just wrap each in foil, freeze and, when ready to use, uncover and bake (Don't thaw first.). Or, the day the soufflés are assembled, they can be held in the refrigerator for a couple of hours before baking.

> 2 tablespoons ($\frac{1}{4}$ stick) unsalted butter
> 2 tablespoons all-purpose flour
> 1 cup whole milk
> 8 ounces Toblerone chocolate, dark, semisweet or milk*, chopped
> 1 ounce unsweetened chocolate, chopped
> 3 tablespoons honey
> 4 large eggs (at room temperature), separated
> $\frac{1}{4}$ teaspoon salt
> 1 tablespoons sugar*
> Sliced almonds
> Powdered sugar (optional)

*If using milk-chocolate Toblerone, reduce amount of sugar very slightly.

Butter 6 soufflé dishes or custard cups, and sprinkle with sugar. Arrange the dishes on a large baking sheet.

Melt the butter in a heavy medium saucepan over medium heat. Add the flour; whisk till mixture bubbles, about 2 minutes. Increase heat to medium-high. Gradually whisk in the milk. Whisk until the mixture boils, thickens, and is smooth, about 1 minute. Remove from the heat. Add the Toblerone chocolate, unsweetened chocolate, and honey; and whisk until melted and smooth. Pour into a large bowl. Cool to room temperature, stirring occasionally.

Preheat oven to 400 degrees.

Whisk the yolks into the chocolate mixture. Beat the whites and salt in medium bowl until soft peaks form. Add 1 tablespoon (or slightly less, if milk-chocolate is used) of sugar; beat until stiff and glossy. Fold $\frac{1}{4}$ of the whites into the chocolate mixture. Gently fold in the remaining whites. Divide the mixture equally among the prepared dishes. Sprinkle the almonds over soufflés.

Bake the soufflés until puffed and almost firm to the touch, but with a center that still moves slightly. If desired, dust the soufflés with powdered sugar before serving, and pass lightly sweetened whipped cream or custard sauce to accompany the soufflés.

Makes 6 1 $\frac{1}{4}$-cup servings.

Bookmarked for Murder is the first in Marion Moore Hill's planned "Sassy Librarian" series. Her story, "Bear With Me," appeared in the anthology *Almostly Murder…With Pets*. She welcomes visitors at www.marionmoorehill.com.

Tart Tatin

CARA BLACK

Aimée walked through the long shadows cast across the courtyard of Hotel Sully. Dark green hedgerows manicured thinly into fleur-de-lys shapes broke up the wide gravel expanse. This tall mansion, another restored hotel particulier, gave access to Place des Vosges via a narrow passageway. A buttery caramel aroma drifted across the courtyard. Her mind darted to the warm, upside-down tart tatin apple tart for which Ma Bourgoyne (a bistro) was famous. The restaurant lay past this narrow passage, under the shadowy arcade of Place des Vosges.
—from *Murder in the Marais*

Recipe Disclaimer: *This is a French recipe, which means butter…Lots of it.*

This caramelized apple tart was created by the Tatin sisters in Orléans. Legend has it that in trying to repair a baking error, they ended up with the renowned upside-down desert.

Crust

    2 ¼ cups unbleached white flour
    1 teaspoon salt
    12 tablespoons unsalted butter, at room temperature
    6 tablespoons water
    12 tablespoons unsalted butter, chilled

Combine the flour and salt in a large bowl. Add the room temperature butter, and cut in, using a pastry blender or fingers, until the mixture resembles coarse meal. Using a fork, stir in the water. Knead the mixture in the bowl, gently, until just smooth dough forms. Shape into a rectangle, wrap in plastic, and chill in the fridge for 1 hour.

Cut the chilled butter into 9 equal pieces. Arrange the pieces side by side on waxed paper, forming a square. Cover with a second sheet of waxed paper. Pound the butter several times with a rolling pin to make it more pliable. Peel off the waxed paper and break into pieces.

Roll out the dough on a floured surface to a 9-by-5-inch rectangle. Turn so that one short side faces you. Arrange the butter pieces evenly over the lower 6 inches of dough. Fold the unbuttered 3 inches of dough over half of unbuttered dough. Fold the remaining 3 inches of buttered dough over, folding as for a letter. Roll out to 12-by-18-inch rectangle. Fold the short sides over to meet in center, then fold in half in the same direction, forming an approximately 12-by-4 ½-inch rectangle. Repeat rolling to 12-by-18-inch rectangle and folding to 12-by-4 ½-inch rectangle. Wrap in plastic and chill.

Filling

¼ cup unsalted butter
¾ cup sugar
12 red apples (Fuji or Gala), peeled, quartered, and cored

Melt the butter in a heavy ovenproof 10-inch skillet—cast iron is good—over medium-high heat. Add the sugar, and stir until sugar melts and the mixture is golden brown. Remove from the heat. Arrange half of the apples, rounded side down, in concentric circles in the skillet. Place the remaining apples cut side down atop the first layers of apples. Cover the skillet. Simmer over low heat until the apples are almost tender, about 25 minutes. Uncover the skillet. Increase heat to medium-low, simmer until the apples are very tender and liquid is reduced to ¼ cup of syrup on the bottom of pan, pressing the apples down into the liquid occasionally, about 45 minutes.

Meanwhile, preheat the oven to 400 degrees.

Cut the dough in half. Let 1 piece stand at room temperature until slightly softened, about 15 minutes. Freeze the second piece of dough for future use. Roll out the dough to a 12-inch diameter round. Place the dough atop the hot apples in the skillet. Trim edge, leaving generous overhang. Fold overhang down tightly around apples. Cut several slits in the dough to allow steam to escape.

Bake the tart until the crust is golden, about 45 minutes. Let cool 5 minutes. Run a small knife around the edge of skillet to loosen tart. Place a large platter over skillet and, using oven mitts, grasp the platter and skillet, and invert, letting the tart settle onto the platter. Carefully lift off the skillet.

Eat and enjoy!

Cara Black's mystery series, set in Paris, includes the Anthony and Macavity-nominated *Murder in the Marais, Murder in Belleville,* and the Anthony Award nominee *Murder in the Sentier.* Sample a bit of France at www.carablack.com.

Katie's Tip Tops

(A Recipe Worth Killing For)

CLAIRE JOHNSON

During my ten years as a pastry chef, I found myself returning more and more to very simple recipes that didn't require a million little steps or weren't constructed with caramel cages or chocolate doodads. In my opinion, these little pastries are what baking is all about. There are no fancy ingredients; it doesn't get more basic than butter, eggs, flour, and jam. And if strawberries are out of season, they are pretty darn delicious with just the whipped cream. These tartlets are best accompanied by a big mug of really strong, sweet tea.

The "Katie" in this recipe is the name of a good friend's Irish grandmother, who won her grandson's heart by making these lovely little tartlets for him.

Preheat the oven to 350 degrees.

Equipment: 22 2 ½ -inch wide, ¾-inch tall tartlet pans

Pastry

2 cups all-purpose flour
¾ teaspoon salt
1 tablespoon sugar
8 tablespoons cold butter (1 stick)
6 tablespoons cold shortening
5 to 6 tablespoons water

Combine the flour, salt, and sugar with a whip. Cut the butter and shortening into the flour mixture until the butter/shortening chunks are peas-size. Add water and incorporate into the flour mixture with a fork. Bring the mixture together with your hands and on a floured board, knead into a ball. Let rest in refrigerator for at least 1 hour.

On a floured board, roll out dough until ⅛-inch thick. Using a 3-inch round cutter, cut out 22 rounds. Fit into tartlet pans and return to the refrigerator to chill while making the filling.

Filling

7 tablespoons all purpose flour
½ teaspoon baking powder
2 eggs
6 tablespoons soft butter
7 tablespoons sugar
Strawberry jam

Combine the flour and baking powder. Set aside. Lightly whip the eggs. Set aside.

Cream together the butter and sugar until light and fluffy. Incorporate the eggs slowly until the mixture comes together. Fold in the flour mixture by hand with a whip.

Remove the tartlets from refrigerator and fill the bottom of each one with ¼ teaspoon strawberry jam. Then top with a very rounded teaspoon of filling.

Place in the oven and bake for 25 minutes or until the tops are golden brown.

Assembling Tip Tops:

   ¾ cup whipping cream
   1 tablespoon sugar
   1 basket strawberries

Whip the cream and sugar together to soft peak. Place the whipping cream in pastry bag and pipe a rosette on top of each tartlet, covering the top of the tartlet. Slice the strawberries into quarters and place 2 pieces on top of each tartlet, sort of like a wing.

These are truly delicious!

Claire M. Johnson's debut mystery, *Beat Until Stiff,* was an Agatha nominee. Learn more at www.rouxmorgue.com.

Apple Pasty

PATRICIA WYNN

*I*t would take the Iron Chef to concoct most of the recipes used in early 18th century England, the setting of my Blue Satan mystery series. Not only are the ingredients unfamiliar to us ("Take your tongue or udder and parboil it…", "Bone and skin your swan…", "Case your reels and gut them…", "Take a quantity of pigs' ears…"), the quantities used also defy the imagination ("Take a hundred and half of large oysters…", "twelve pigeons…", "six gallons of your bloody beef-brine", "twelve pounds of lean beef, cut in thin slices… in a stew pan over the fire…"). I don't know about you, but my stew pan doesn't hold twelve pounds of beef. Today's homemaker, too, lacks the essential muscles to beat ingredients for—I kid you not—up to two hours.

One of the only reasonable recipes I can offer, therefore, while a little heavy in cholesterol, at least has recognizable elements and is still enjoyed today. In some circumstances, it may also be used as a murder weapon. Be sure to keep the temperature of your kitchen cold, and prepare to get messy.

To make puff-paste for tarts:

Work ¼ pound of butter into 1 pound of fine flour; then whip the whites of 2 eggs to snow, and with cold water and 1 yolk make it into a paste. Roll it out on a floured board, and gradually put in a second pound of butter by spreading a layer of butter over the dough, flouring over the butter, rolling or folding it up, then rolling the dough out again. It will take 6 or 7 times to work in all the butter. Roll out and cut into shapes for filling.

This puff-pastry can be filled with seasoned, stewed meat or stewed fruit before frying in oil.

Filling for apple pasties:

Pare and quarter apples (I would guess about 6 apples would do*). Boil them in sugar (½ to ⅔ cup) and water with a stick of cinnamon. When tender, season to taste with a little white wine, juice of a lemon, fresh butter, and ambergris**, or orange-flower water. Stir all together, and when it is cold, put a small amount in a puff-paste. Fold over and pinch closed. Fry in oil.

Warning: People in the 18th century walked, carried, and, yes, whipped batter for two hours straight. That's why they got to eat like this. They also died young.

*I got this recipe from a 17th century cookbook and they didn't have measurings cups and spoons. Experiment with quantities if desired.

**Helpful Hint: If ambergris is not readily available a little honey with cinnamon may be substituted.

Patricia Wynn is the author of the Blue Satan Mystery Series, which includes *The Birth of Blue Satan* and *The Spider's Touch*.

Buttered Oranges

JANET LAURENCE

This is a modern version of a delicious seventeenth century dish. I included it on the table of historical food in the first scene of the first Darina Lisle culinary mystery, *A Deepe Coffyn*. It attracted one reader in particular, a chef, who felt any book that included so noteworthy a dish had to be worth reading! The dish was originally made with Seville oranges, with a greater proportion of sugar. The bitter oranges would have given a much richer flavor. One Seville orange added instead of one of the sweet oranges would improve the flavor of this recipe but the peel needs to be boiled first to remove some of the bitterness. The dish does not have to be served in the orange shells, you could use small dishes instead, but they make a nice presentation.

Michael Smith, a prominent English cookery writer who was deeply interested in traditional dishes, deserves the credit for rediscovering this recipe.

8 small, thin skinned oranges
(6 to be used as containers)
5 large egg yolks
4 tablespoons caster sugar
1 tablespoon orange liqueur

1 stick unsalted butter, diced
Generous ½ cup double/heavy cream
Large piece candied orange peel, chopped,
or peel of 1 orange crystallised and drained*

Cut off the tops of six of the oranges, about three-quarters of an inch below the blossom end—a serrated or scalloped pattern looks nice. Scoop out the pulp (this is not used in the recipe and can be saved, squeezed and used for drinking, orange jelly, or whatever). Grate the peel of the 2 remaining oranges. Place with their juice in a bowl over a pan of simmering water, or use a double boiler, then add the yolks and sugar, and beat until pale and thick. Remove from heat, place the bowl in iced water to stop further cooking, add the liqueur and butter, and stir in. Beat the mixture until smooth and cold. Whip the cream until floppy but not at all stiff, fold into orange mixture. Add the candied or crystallised orange peel, folding in carefully. Then fill the orange shells with buttered orange mixture and replace lids. Chill either in a plastic bag or box or wrapped in cling film.

Serves 6.

*Crystallised orange peel: Remove the peel from oranges without pith; shred or cut or leave whole. Bring to a boil in cold water, drain, refresh in cold water, then repeat process. Melt 10 tablespoons caster sugar in 5 tablespoons water, bring to boil, simmer for 2 minutes then add the peel, and cook gently for 5 minutes. Leave to cool. Use as required. Shreds of crystallised orange peel transform a plain orange salad, especially with a little orange liqueur; the syrup can be used to sweeten a fresh fruit salad or with strawberries and double cream for ice cream.

Janet Laurence's culinary mysteries include: *A Deepe Coffyn, Appetite for Death* and *The Mermaid's Feast.*

Apple Crisp

LIBBY FISCHER HELLMANN

*E*llie Foreman is a single mom and video producer who lives on the North Shore of Chicago. Ellie dispensed with the idea of cooking perfectly balanced, nutritional meals a long time ago. (Particularly after her divorce.) In fact, Ellie's definition of the four major food groups would include: Chocolate, pizza, wine, and chocolate. However, since this is a collection of recipes that some people might actually use to feed their families, she offers this somewhat nutritional, non-chocolate dessert. The key to it, aside from being delicious, is that it's a *No Brainer*. It's really easy. She wouldn't have it any other way. Plus, if anyone is keeping kosher, it can be easily made parve.

> 1 stick butter or margarine
> 6 apples, peeled, sliced, and cored—okay, that's the time consuming part
> 1 cup sugar
> 1 cup flour

Set out the butter or margarine till soft. Preheat the oven to 350 degrees.

Core, slice, and peel the apples, and place them in a baking dish. Wash hands and mix the butter/margarine, flour, and sugar, by hand, until crumbly. Sprinkle on top of the apples. Bake for 30 to 40 minutes.

Serve with whipped cream, vanilla ice cream, or go bare.

Ellie Foreman made her debut in Libby Fischer Hellmann's *An Eye for Murder* and continues her adventures in *A Picture of Guilt.*

Index

Jo Grossman is the former proprietor of The Mystery Café, a mystery bookstore/café that combined her love of good food and good crime novels, in Sheffield, Massachusetts. She worked in film and television for many years, including a three-year stint on *In the Heat of the Night*. She lives in Massachusetts.

Robert Weibezahl is a writer and publicist. A monthly book review columnist for *BookPage*, his articles on books and culture have also appeared in *Mystery Readers Journal*, *Irish America* magazine, the *Los Angeles Daily News*, the *Los Angeles Reader*, and the *Dictionary of Literary Biography Yearbook*. He lives in California.

To receive a free catalog of other Poisoned Pen Press titles,
please contact us in one of the follow ing ways:

Phone: 1-800-421-3976
Facsimile: 1-480-949-1707
Email: info@poisonedpenpress.com
Website: www.poisonedpenpress.com

Poisoned Pen Press
6962 E. First Ave. Ste 103
Scottsdale, AZ 85251